capture your call

capture your call

Accepting
God's challenge
for our lives

Terry-Anne Preston

Text copyright © Terry-Anne Preston 1999

The author asserts the moral right
to be identified as the author of this work

Published by
The Bible Reading Fellowship
Peter's Way, Sandy Lane West
Oxford OX4 5HG
ISBN 1 84101 083 9

First published 1999
1 3 5 7 9 10 8 6 4 2 0

Acknowledgments

Unless otherwise stated, scripture quotations are taken from The
New Revised Standard Version of the Bible, Anglicized Edition,
copyright © 1989, 1995 by the Division of Christian Education of
the National Council of the Churches of Christ in the USA, and are
used by permission. All rights reserved.

The Holy Bible, New International Version, copyright © 1973, 1978,
1984 by International Bible Society. Used by permission of Hodder
& Stoughton Limited. All rights reserved. 'NIV' is a registered
trademark of International Bible Society. UK trademark number
1448790.

Scripture quotations from the New Jerusalem Bible, published and
copyright © 1985 by Darton, Longman and Todd Ltd and les
Editions du Cerf, and by Doubleday, a division of Bantam Doubleday
Dell Publishing Group, Inc. Used by permission of Darton,
Longman and Todd Ltd, and Doubleday, a division of Random
House, Inc.

A catalogue record for this book is available from the British Library

Printed and bound in Great Britain by
Caledonian Book Manufacturing International, Glasgow

This book is dedicated to the fond memory of Doris and Chris Foy and Edith and Reg Benefer

Acknowledgments

I wonder if you are reading this acknowledgment in the hope that your name, or that of someone you know, will be listed. If so, read on... because you might, indeed, be here.

Many authors seem to state the same but, in respect of *Capture Your Call*, there are a great many people to thank for helping me to write this book. They range from my sister, Lisa, who allowed me to print a highly embarrassing story about her; through to Elaine and Lyndsey who proofread the original manuscript. They include my spiritual director and his colleagues (who allow me to escape every few months to a delightful telephone-free zone), the trustees and supporters of The Framework Trust (who helped to create the time for writing as well as much-needed prayer support) and my prayer partner of the last ten years, Di.

Perhaps, though, the biggest acknowledgment should, on this occasion, go to Kath Semple. Without her, and her openness to the prompting of the Holy Spirit, this book—as you will discover—could not have been completed.

Contents

Introduction

Friends of mine recently acquired a new telephone. It is a model that displays the number of the person calling as the phone is ringing. A marvellous invention! It allows the person being called to see in advance who it is at the other end and then to make an informed decision as to whether or not to answer the call.

The call of God, however, does not always come with a caller display message attached. Many Christians say that they long to hear God speak to them directly, to hear his voice and to know what it is that he wants them to do. Yet often God speaks to us quietly, without loud ringing bells or writing on the wall. He seldom demands that we speak to him but often prefers to invite us quietly to chat. Sometimes he speaks to us so gently that we do not even realize who it is that is speaking to us. And sometimes, even though we can spend years complaining that God does not seem to be making his voice heard, when we do hear it we wish that we had not. Occasionally, we may see with total clarity that God has a plan for us, yet we deliberately choose not to answer.

If you identify with any of these reactions, take comfort in the fact that many of the best-known characters in the Bible reacted to the call of God in similar ways. Moses argued with God; Jeremiah complained about his lack of experience and qualifications; and Jonah even tried to run away! Yet today the life of each of these people is a model and example to us all. This is because they learned to trust God and to accept his judgment in calling them. They overcame their fears, doubts and inadequacies and attempted to capture the call for which they had been anointed.

The Bible contains many examples of how God calls a wide range of people. He speaks to them in a variety of ways and calls them to vastly different tasks and roles. Scripture makes it clear that God loves to call each person to a unique role. Yet today, the subject of calling is often mistakenly reserved for those entering some kind of 'full-time' Christian commitment. Clergy, members of religious communities or missionaries may be taught a little about the meaning of 'a call'. But the rest of us can live in a kind of spiritual vacuum, hoping that we are doing the right things but never being very certain that we are.

Capture your Call starts by looking at some of the best-known and best-loved characters in the Bible, exploring the ways in which God spoke to them and made his call known, and then identifying the reaction of each individual to that call.

But this is not a book about others. This is a book about us. What can we learn from the Bible characters? Which reaction do we most identify with, and why? And most importantly, how can we hear the call of God for our life, overcome our fears and concerns and then step out to fulfil our call? It is unlikely that God will call every one of us to a dramatic change of lifestyle; after all, we cannot all immediately become missionaries in Africa! But we can experience the call of God even if we are already in the right place; and a clear call can give us an increased sense of vision and purpose for the things in which we are already involved. Calling affects our family situation as well as our job; it influences our play times as well as our church life; it has as much to do with our relationships as with our finances.

Capture Your Call invites us to accept a challenge—the challenge of picking up the phone when the caller display panel reveals that it is God who wishes to speak with us. Will we accept the challenge? Will we attempt to capture our call?

Section
one

Biblical calls and responses

Jonah—The man who ran away

Key verse

Now the word of the Lord came to Jonah son of Amittai, saying, 'Go at once to Nineveh, that great city, and cry out against it; for their wickedness has come up before me.' But Jonah set out to flee to Tarshish from the presence of the Lord. He went down to Joppa and found a ship going to Tarshish; so he paid his fare and went on board, to go with them to Tarshish, away from the presence of the Lord.

JONAH 1:1–3

Suggested reading: Jonah 1—4

Not long after I had become a Christian, I heard God speaking to me. At the time I did not realize that that was who it was but, looking back, it has become clear that it was indeed God speaking.

I was sitting alone in my flat and the words 'Write to John' kept going round and round my head. If it had been another name, I would probably have assumed that I had forgotten to write to someone, but I did not actually know anyone called John. The only person I had met with that name was a friend of a friend of mine. We had only ever exchanged half a dozen words, and all I knew about him was that he was a dancer. I pushed aside all thoughts of writing and told myself I was making it up. In an attempt to cover up the words that were becoming more and more forceful, I made myself busy. I cleaned the flat as it had never been cleaned before. I went shopping and filled the cupboards from top to bottom. I ironed every single item in the ironing basket. Every task that had been waiting for months to be completed was finished that Saturday afternoon. Eventually I sat down with a cup of coffee, and still the words were buzzing round my head.

Being a new Christian, I did not know the Bible very well. No one had told me which verse to look up when you have persistent thoughts of writing letters to strangers! I opened the Bible at random—or so I thought—and came across this verse: 'Be doers of the word and not merely hearers who deceive themselves' (James 1:22). That was clear enough to propel me towards the desk in order to find paper and pen. But what to write? I prayed that if this really was something that he wanted me to do, God would show me what to write. I picked up the pen and wrote... and wrote... and wrote. I did not stop until I reached the end of the letter. Still feeling somewhat foolish and uncertain about what I was doing, I folded the letter without reading it, and put it in an envelope, writing the name on the front. It was only then that I realized that I did not know where John lived. Confident that the letter would simply sit on the desk until I eventually moved house and threw it away, I went to bed. The next morning, the letter had gone. My flatmate had been in, seen it sitting on the desk and had taken it with her as she went out early in the morning to a meeting where she knew John would be present. How embarrassing! Now I knew that I had made a fool of myself! I resolved to keep myself hidden—staying away from anywhere that John or his friends might go.

After a week, I was starting to recover and had just about managed to put the whole incident to the back of my mind. Then the post arrived. There was a letter from John. 'How glad I am that you wrote when you did,' it started. I could not believe it. I had thought he would assume that I'd gone mad! He went on, though, to explain that on the day he received my letter he had been to the doctor. An injury he sustained while dancing had turned out to be more serious than was first thought. The dance company had terminated his contract immediately, claiming that he was no longer fit for work and was unlikely ever to recover fully. He was unemployed, penniless and had no idea what to do with his life now that his dream of dancing had been shattered. My letter had been sitting in his pocket throughout the day and it was only late that night, in the midst of deep despair, that he had opened it. He told me that the verse from Jeremiah I had quoted had deeply affected him. It had restored his faith and reminded him of the fact that God knew about his situation and was in control of it. I looked up the verse (using the index because I had not even heard of Jeremiah!) and read, 'Surely I know the plans I have for you, says the

Lord, plans for your welfare and not for harm, to give you a future with hope' (Jeremiah 29:11).

How grateful I was then that God had been persistent in his speaking to me! All I had wanted to do was to ignore him—to busy myself with other things that would take my mind off the one thing that God actually wanted me to do.

In a similar way, Jonah heard God speaking to him. Wow! The creator of the whole universe was speaking clearly to this one man. Not only that, but he too was being given a very specific job to do. But how did Jonah respond? He ran away! Despite recognizing the personal call of God, he tried to go as far away as possible. He deliberately set out to 'flee… from the presence of the Lord' (Jonah 1:3). And he didn't just take a few small steps along the wrong path, he turned around and went in completely the opposite direction! His aim was to get as far away as possible—not just from the task to which he was being called, but from God himself.

The story of Jonah

The story of Jonah is a familiar one. God asks Jonah to go to Nineveh in order to preach against the evil that was there. Jonah runs off and boards a ship that he knows is going in the opposite direction. A great storm occurs, causing the crew to panic and to cast lots in order to find out who is responsible for the desperate situation in which they find themselves. The lot identifies Jonah, who tells the sailors to throw him overboard. This they do, the storm abates and God sends a huge fish to swallow Jonah and take him to shore. Having recognized his initial failure to obey God's call to him, Jonah then does as he is asked the second time and goes to Nineveh. The people—including the king— hear, via Jonah, God's call to repentance and they declare a fast, resolving to turn away from evil. Jonah then becomes angry. Very angry. He tells God that he knew this would happen and he asks to die. Twice God challenges him about his right to be angry but Jonah appears to retain his anger. The story ends with God reiterating his love for the people of Nineveh.

God's provision

Whilst we may not always recognize it at the time, obedience often allows us to see more clearly God's provision for us. Running away may mean that we end up having to do more than God actually intended for us to do. This is certainly true in the case of Jonah. He went to Joppa and found—possibly after a lot of searching—a ship headed for Tarshish. He then paid the fare. When the word of the Lord came to Jonah a second time and he obeyed by travelling to Nineveh, there is no suggestion that Jonah needed to pay for anything. When he was thrown into the sea and needed to get to land, he had no difficulty in finding free transport, as a large fish was provided. And when he needed shade later on, God provided a vine just for him. All free of charge! God clearly cared about Jonah to such an extent that he wanted to provide just what he needed, but Jonah did not seem to realize this. He was definitely not keen to do as God had asked; not at first.

Why did Jonah flee?

Many of us long to hear the voice of God clearly speaking to us. It seems incredible to those of us who seldom experience this, that someone who does hear a specific call could contemplate running away. What prompted Jonah's action? Why, after hearing God speaking to him, did Jonah refuse to do as he was asked and run away?

We cannot be certain as to exactly why Jonah ran away but the Bible story hints at four possible grade 'A' reasons:

- **Afraid**
- **Attachments**
- **Arrogance**
- **Alternatives**

Afraid

Jonah may well have experienced fear. When we know that we have a task to do, our mind automatically leaps ahead and considers all the possible outcomes. Jonah was surely no exception. How would the people of Nineveh react when he told them that God saw their wickedness? Would they believe that the message actually came from

God? Or would they attack the messenger? It may have been a clear calling but it certainly was not an easy message to give.

Attachments

After speaking to the Ninevites, Jonah tells God what his thoughts had been 'while I was still in my own country' (Jonah 4:2). Perhaps Jonah had become accustomed to being at home, in familiar surroundings. It can be hard to leave behind those things that have become precious to us. Any person who spends a great deal of time away from home will be able to list the things they miss. Usually these are not the big things but the tiny things that most of us seldom really take note of: spring flowers, familiar-smelling soap, a good cup of tea! Even when we know that it is God who is calling us, we still have to weigh up the cost of leaving behind the things, and indeed the people, that we have learned to hold dear.

Arrogance

Jonah may be the story of a man who knew and heard God but he is also a man struggling with pride. He is proud of his faith in God and this comes through when the sailors ask him to explain himself (1:9). He is proud of his ability to remember God when he is buried inside the fish and in great distress (2:7). And he even has the audacity to argue with God about his rights (4:9). Perhaps most importantly, however, Jonah thought so little of the Ninevites that he actually did not want them to go unpunished—he wanted God to judge them harshly (4:1). This, along with the action of running away, shows Jonah to be a man who struggled in the area of submission. He could not submit his whole life to God.

Alternatives

Jonah thought that he knew better than God. He thought that the Ninevites deserved to be punished, and he had such a high view of his own role that he believed that, if he did not warn the Ninevites, God would have no choice but to punish them. One minute he is proclaiming how well he knows God: 'For I knew that you are a gracious God and merciful, slow to anger, and abounding in steadfast love, and ready to relent from punishing' (4:2). The next minute, he is angry at God's seeming lack of concern about him: 'O Lord, please take my life from me, for it is better for me to die than to live' (4:3). He does not seem to realize at all that God loved the Ninevites too—so much so, that if Jonah had not obeyed his call God would certainly have raised up someone else to warn and rescue them.

Throughout the story, Jonah's focus is on how God is using him to speak to the Ninevites rather than on what God wants to do in Jonah himself. He wrongly thinks that God is more interested in what he does than in who he is.

What was the effect of Jonah's actions?

The consequences of our actions can be far-reaching. None of us lives in total isolation, and our decisions are bound to affect other people.

- **The people of Nineveh had to wait for Jonah to arrive. If he had obeyed God the first time, he would have arrived much earlier and the people might have repented sooner. God wanted to save the Ninevites from the consequences of their own sinful actions: the sooner Jonah reached them, the sooner they would be out of danger.**
- **The sailors were also put into danger. 'Then the mariners were afraid, and each cried to his god' (1:5). Up until the time they threw Jonah overboard, they struggled with their consciences, desperate to do the right thing, yet uncertain as to what that was.**
- **Jonah is himself challenged by God throughout the story. Having waited patiently for Jonah to make his mistakes, God provides every possible means to help him get back on the right track. He calms the storm, he provides a big fish, he reiterates the original call he gave to Jonah, he provides the vine to give shade and he provides the worm and the hot sun to teach Jonah an important lesson.**

Above all, this is a story of God's love for human beings. He loves whole communities even when they are steeped in sin and evil; and he loves the individual—even when he or she runs away.

Are we people who run away?

This may seem like a funny question to ask. Do we run away? In the physical sense, of course, most of us do not run away. We are rooted in churches, homes and communities, and no matter what situations arise, or how difficult things become, we are usually on hand to deal with them and see things through to a conclusion of some kind.

But there is more to this story than the physical aspect of running— keen as Jonah was to do that. This is the story of a man who heard God asking him to do something but who was reluctant to do it. We need to explore these two aspects in relation to our own lives.

God's call is specific

Few people seem to hear God speaking to them as clearly and as specifically as Jonah appeared to. Yet God has a specific plan for each one of us. Jeremiah 29:11, as quoted previously, states: 'For surely I know the plans I have for you, says the Lord, plans for your welfare and not for harm, to give you a future with hope.' God may not call us to a task as daunting as the one Jonah received but he does have something for each person that is clear, specific and challenging. So how do we discover more of God's plan for our lives?

A reluctance to obey

The Bible makes it clear that we must take action as well as listening to the word of God: 'Be doers of the word and not merely hearers who deceive themselves' (James 1:22). Hearing our call, on its own, is not enough. God wants us to obey his every word, doing what he asks and constantly moving forward into the new challenges he has for us. Are we ready to do that? Or, like Jonah, are there things that hold us back?

Five steps to discover our calling

JONAH can help us discover what it is that God wants us to do today.

J is for Jesus

Jonah heard the word of God. He listened to it. He may not have obeyed it initially but he certainly heard it. Are we spending time learning how to listen to God? Most of us have a nagging doubt every time there is the possibility that God has spoken to us: Was that really God? Is he really speaking to me? Have I heard him correctly? These can be good questions to ask, keeping us humble and dependent on God but as we grow in our relationship with Jesus—via prayer, Bible study, worship and fellowship with other Christians—we will gradually learn how to discern more clearly the voice of God.

Let's use the model Jesus gave us to look at our own pattern of private prayer, Bible study, worship and fellowship with other Christians. Do we rely solely on the church to provide these things? Or are they a part of our normal everyday life from Monday to Saturday, as well as on Sunday?

- **Private prayer:** Like Jesus, we need to build into our prayer times a period of silence, asking God to speak to us and maybe writing down what we feel he says. If it is appropriate to do so, we can share our writings and thoughts with a close friend. Learning how to listen to God together may help us to build our confidence in hearing him for ourselves.
- **Bible study:** Jesus knew the scriptures well and we, too, need to get to know the Bible. Daily reading, maybe with helpful notes to guide us, is an invaluable tool as we seek to learn more of God's character and plan for our lives.
- **Worship:** Many Christians find corporate worship much easier than worshipping when alone. Yet learning how to worship God at all times, and in all places, just as Jesus did, will help us to keep God's perspective in any situation where we find ourselves. The book of Psalms is very helpful in this respect—just reading aloud Psalms such as 33 and 34 will help us as we start to explore personal worship.
- **Fellowship with other Christians:** Jesus took time to be with other people. Even when he was particularly busy or had large numbers of people making demands on him, he made a point of finding time to be with his disciples, as well as creating time alone with God. If fellowship was so important for Jesus, how much more important should it be for us.

O is for Others

It was only when he was in real trouble on the ship, and was being questioned by the sailors, that Jonah was able to see the truth of his situation. Those around him challenged him, until he could say, 'I worship the Lord, the God of heaven, who made the sea and the dry land' (1:9). He was honest with them and admitted that he was running away.

We were created to be part of a community. We were never intended to be alone. God has placed us in churches and communities through which we can rely on each other to help discern and test God's call on our life.

Do we try to work out God's call for our life alone? This can be difficult and sometimes dangerous. It is hard to be objective when we are thinking, questioning and listening for ourselves. Jonah did not like what he heard and it was only after being challenged by the sailors that he ultimately came to recognize his need to follow God's call and not his own will.

We need to ask God to show us one or two people with whom we can honestly test out the things we feel God is asking us to do. These may be people from our church or home group, from our family or place of work. Sometimes God brings us together with surprising people—the sailors who confronted Jonah were the last people he would have expected to help him discover God's plan. We should not look for people who will always agree with our point of view. We need to find people who will question us, challenge us, be honest with us— even when that means that they have to tell us we could be wrong.

Other people will often be able to see our abilities, gifts and calling much more clearly than we are able to do ourselves. If we start to sense God calling us to lead a children's group for example, others may be able to see how God has been preparing us for that over the years. They may be able to recall times we have spent with their children, or helpful things we learned when we were children ourselves.

N is for Now

No matter how strongly we feel called to a task, timing is almost always difficult to work out. The story of Jonah implies that he acted as soon as he heard the word but this is not altogether certain from the text. Sometimes God starts to speak to us about a task or role many years before it takes place. Impatience or disbelief then gets in the way. 'How could God have said that when it hasn't happened yet?' 'Maybe I should give up my job, sell my house and make it happen now!'

Vision is vital. We all need something to aim for—a goal in our life. Without it, we easily lose our way. The New Jerusalem Bible has an interesting translation for Proverbs 29:18: 'Where there is no vision the people get out of hand.'

We need three kinds of call or vision:

- **Our lifetime call to become more Christ-like, growing in love for God and for each other. This call will encourage us in our prayer life, our Bible study and our attendance at and participation in the life of the church.**
- **A long-term call that will provide an overall direction to where God wants us to be and what he wants us to do. Maybe he is calling us to be a parent or a pastor, a postman or a potter, a politician or a physician. For each of us the call will be specific and unique, specially tailored by God for us.**
- **An immediate call to serve God and the people around us now, in whatever situation we currently find ourselves.**

All three aspects of calling are needed in order to ensure that we live balanced lives and live them to the full. A long-term call to be a missionary in Mongolia may be great and fulfilling when we are there; but what about the years before and afterwards? What about the furloughs and the days off? Can God not teach us and use us then? Of course he can! As the song accurately states, he has the whole of our lives in his hands, not just little bits and pieces.

Our immediate call may not appear to be linked to our long-term call. Parents, for example, who give up careers and church roles in order to bring up children, can sometimes feel frustrated that they are not physically able to do some of the other things they feel called to do. Jonah was asked to preach against Nineveh. Yet of all the forty-eight verses in the story, he actually preaches in only one of them. Does this mean that for ninety-eight per cent of the time he was unfruitful and of no interest to God? Of course not! It simply shows that God spent ninety-eight per cent of his time looking after Jonah, caring about his every need and teaching him how to become more like God himself, and only two per cent of the time letting him work in this way. What a loving God!

A is for Accept

Hearing God is one thing. Obeying is quite another! When we hear God speak to us, we need to accept what he says and put it into practice.

Probably the greatest moment of distress for Jonah was when he was inside the fish. It was at this point that he turned to God in prayer. As we accept God's call to us, we also can pray part of Jonah's prayer:

Those who cling to worthless idols
forfeit the grace that could be theirs.
But I, with a song of thanksgiving,
will sacrifice to you.
What I have vowed I will make good.
Salvation comes from the Lord.
JONAH 2:8–9 (NIV)

It might be helpful to meditate on these words, taking them to heart and learning them so that we can recall them at times when it is particularly appropriate to do so.

In order to accept God's call to us, we need to free ourselves from the things that bind us like Jonah:

- **Afraid?** Are we afraid to step out and trust God? 'There is no fear in love, but perfect love casts out fear; for fear has to do with punishment, and whoever fears has not reached perfection in love' (1 John 4:18). We need to voice our fears before God, recognizing them and trusting that he will help us to overcome them.
- **Attachments?** What holds us back? The love of money? Our home? Our routine? Family? Friends? Church? We need to give these to God in prayer, being honest about the things that hold us.

- **Arrogance?** Are we prepared to submit our whole life to Christ? Or are we prepared to let him take charge of only part of our lives?
- **Alternatives?** Do we think that God made a mistake when he called us? Maybe when he created us? God knows what he is doing. If he is asking us to do something, he has his own reasons for choosing us. And he has chosen us: 'You did not choose me but I chose you. And I appointed you to go and bear fruit, fruit that will last, so that the Father will give you whatever you ask him in my name' (John 15:16).

H is for Honour

When we do step out and obey God, he often does amazing things. Look how the whole city of Nineveh reacted when Jonah was obedient. Whatever we do, we need to ensure that the resulting glory, honour and praise go to God. This is not always easy to do in practice. Many of us either fail to recognize God's hand in the things that happen around us, or believe that it is only God who works and that our part was not important. We need to learn to get the balance right—playing our part to the full, yet giving the ultimate honour to God, who equips us and enables us to co-operate with him.

Questions for personal consideration or group discussion

1. Can you recall ever running away from God or from something that he asked you to do? Why did you respond in the way you did? What did you learn through that experience?

2. Are there things that you are putting off doing? Writing a letter? Making a telephone call? Visiting a friend? Can you resolve now to meet those tasks in the coming week?

3. Do you believe that God is more interested in what you do than in who you are? If you could correct this belief, what practical difference would this make to you on a day-by-day basis?

4. How can God speak to you, use you, love you, today? What might he be saying to you about your gifts and your long-term calling? Look back and see how far he has brought you in your lifetime call to become more Christ-like. Pray through the three aspects of your personal calling, thanking him for everything that he has given and taught you, and for the fact that he loves you.

5. Work through the four 'A's, identifying your fears, attachments, arrogance and alternatives. Are there additional things that might be preventing you from accepting God's call?

Jeremiah—A childlike response

Key verse

'Ah, Lord God! Truly I do not know how to speak, for I am only a boy.'
But the Lord said to me, 'Do not say, "I am only a boy."'
JEREMIAH 1:6–7

Suggested reading: Jeremiah 1

As a child, my sister Lisa loved horse-riding. Every week she would go to the local stable for a lesson and, occasionally, I would go with my parents to collect her. On one occasion we arrived before the lesson had finished and saw the end of an informal show-jumping competition between all the students. It ended in a tie for first place between Lisa and her friend. They were asked to participate in a jump-off, with Lisa invited to go first. With great care and attention to detail, she mounted her horse and slowly guided it past all the jumps to the centre of the indoor ring. Then, after a brief pause for effect, and with great style and elegance—she jumped right off the horse!

She had assumed that top marks were to be awarded to the person who managed to dismount in the quickest and most creative way. To the rest of us, it was hilarious! We instantly realized that she had taken the request for a 'jump-off' literally. For her, though, it was devastating. She simply could not understand why the rest of us found it amusing. No one had actually explained to her what the term 'jump-off' meant. Everyone had assumed that she would know. But why should she? How was she—a young child—to know that it should not have been taken literally?

God loves childlike trust and simplicity. Not, of course, because it makes us figures of fun but because it shows that we love and trust him. The childlike quality of being able to say and do exactly what we see and hear—and that alone—is something God recognized as being present in Jeremiah. With God's help, training and encouragement, this childlikeness was transformed from an apparent weakness into a great strength, making him one of the greatest prophets in the Old Testament.

But it nearly did not happen. Jeremiah's reaction when he realized God was calling him was to complain about his lack of experience and qualifications—the one thing that God wanted!

The Old Testament book of Jeremiah contains a mixture of Jeremiah's own life story, a description of the visions and prophecies he received and an outline of the historical situation at the time.

Jeremiah was the son of Hilkiah, who was a priest. As such, it was likely that Jeremiah was subject to teaching about ancient church traditions and he was almost certainly aware of prophets who had gone before him and of the prophecies that they had received. He may have considered becoming a priest himself, but there is no clear confirmation of this in scripture. The first three verses of Jeremiah help to establish that his call to be a prophet took place around 645BC and, overall, his ministry as recorded in scripture lasted approximately forty-five to fifty years—at least fifteen times longer than that of Jesus.

The calling of Jeremiah

The biblical account of the calling of Jeremiah is written as a direct conversation between the potential prophet and God. We cannot know exactly how this conversation took place but what is very clear is that Jeremiah knew that he had been called by God directly.

'The word of the Lord…' (Jeremiah 1:4) is a phrase that recurs many times in the book of Jeremiah. It signifies, both to him and to those who heard and now read his words, the certainty that Jeremiah felt in knowing that what he was about to say did indeed originate from God.

Even without this phrase, though, this calling has the fingerprints of God all over it. God always sees the whole picture and, at the very start of his calling, Jeremiah is given a sense of God's purpose for his life, right from the time of his conception:

Before I formed you in the womb I knew you,
and before you were born I consecrated you;
I appointed you a prophet to the nations.'
JEREMIAH 1: 5

God calls within a context. For Jeremiah, the call is within the context of his whole life and with an awareness of the life-long preparation he has been given for the task to which he is being called. The call is clear and specific—aimed at one man, with one task, to one target group.

How did Jeremiah respond?

With such a clear calling, it might be assumed that Jeremiah's reaction would be one of enthusiasm to get started in his new role! What a commission! Why not get on and do it straightaway?

Of course, this is not how he responded. When faced with the prospect of speaking out for God across the nations, Jeremiah immediately recognized his own inexperience: 'Ah, Lord God! Truly I do not know how to speak, for I am only a boy' (Jeremiah 1:6).

We cannot be sure exactly how old Jeremiah was at this point—he must have been quite young—but this is more than a comment on age. This is a plea from the heart, based on feelings of total inadequacy. Jeremiah is challenging God on his choice of person for the job. He obviously recognized the importance and significance of the role but he was full of self-doubt.

Does this sound familiar? On many occasions in the Bible, and across the world since the Bible was compiled, God calls people to tasks for which they feel under-qualified. This is such a common reaction, in fact, that it is sometimes seen as one of the ways by which we can test a call. If we feel that we can accomplish a task in our own strength, God may not be calling us to do it. He chooses people who will rely on him rather than themselves, and asking someone who feels totally inadequate to do the job for him is likely to ensure that they remain close to God, pursuing God's way rather than their own.

How did God react?

God instantly acknowledged Jeremiah's feelings of inadequacy. He did not ignore them or brush over them. Instead, he confronted them head-on and dealt with them in a way that Jeremiah could cope with:

Do not say, 'I am only a boy';
for you shall go to all to whom I send you,
and you shall speak whatever I command you.
Do not be afraid of them,
for I am with you to deliver you, says the Lord.
JEREMIAH 1:7–8

God promises that he will be with Jeremiah every step of the way; he will show him to whom he is to go and, once there, God will give him the words to say. It is to be a partnership. God and Jeremiah will work together. The call that comes from God is not, as perhaps Jeremiah feared, a call that sends us out to go and get on with the task alone.

This passage is often referred to as the 'commission' of Jeremiah. The 'call' comes first, with God telling Jeremiah the role for which he has been appointed. The 'commission' is the sending out to do it. The nature of commission in our churches today tends often to carry the connotation of being sent away from others—a missionary, for example, is often commissioned by his or her own home church in order to go and work outside the local community. Through Jeremiah, God shows us the importance of commissioning people to work locally as well as more widely afield.

As with many calls, God is quick to dispel fear, telling Jeremiah not to be afraid. Fear is something that the promises of God can dispel, giving us hope that, with his help, it is possible to control our fears. We need to learn to trust God and his provision for us. God is encouraging —or in other words, 'giving courage to'—Jeremiah by promising to guide his every movement and word.

God, though, does not rely solely upon words. Immediately after giving his promise to oversee all that Jeremiah does, God embarks upon a training course with his prodigy. God reaches out and touches Jeremiah's mouth (1:9), anointing him for the task to which he has been called. Then he asks him, 'Jeremiah, what do you see?' Jeremiah replies, 'I see a branch of an almond tree' (1:11).

Jeremiah faithfully replies with an exact description of that which he sees—a branch of an almond tree. This is almost certainly something that Jeremiah sees in his spirit or imagination, an impression that strikes him, rather than a physical almond branch in front of him. Note how the childlike simplicity that caused Jeremiah to protest about his calling is immediately put to good, positive use by God—Jeremiah says what he sees, and that alone. Just as my sister literally did as she was told when she jumped off her horse, in the same way Jeremiah reports what he can see, without interpretation, embellishment or comment. God immediately encourages him: 'You have seen well' (1:12).

This whole process is repeated, with God asking Jeremiah to say what he can see a second time. Again, Jeremiah describes exactly what he can see. The third time, God sends Jeremiah to Jerusalem to speak out against their idolatry and backsliding, confident now that Jeremiah will remain faithful to God, speaking out only what God is giving him.

The word of the Lord came to me, saying:
'Go and proclaim in the hearing of Jerusalem,
Thus says the Lord...'
JEREMIAH 2:1–2

Jeremiah's experience can be summarized as follows:

• **God calls**
• **God commissions**
• **God communicates both verbally and visually**

Are we Jeremiah people?
If God were to call us today to a task as daunting as that of speaking out against wrongdoing, would we react in a similar way to Jeremiah? Would our first reaction be to protest and to point out our lack of experience and qualifications, or would we jump at the opportunity to serve God in whatever way he thought best? Many of us would like the

latter description to mirror our reaction, but in our heart of hearts we know that there would be at least an element of the former in our response. And this reaction is likely to appear even when we are called to less public roles.

When we think back to previous occasions when we have been aware of God's calling, how did we react? Did we find ourselves complaining to God? Or feel inadequate in any way? Did we find that we embellished what God was asking us to do, trying to make things happen in ways that he had not indicated? Or perhaps we refused to speak out at all when he asked us to do so?

Do we complain to God?
For months, maybe for years, we can pray for God to speak to us and lead us, yet when he does our immediate response is to protest. We complain that he does not seem to speak to us when we want him to, and that he does speak to us when we do not want him to. And when he does speak, he often asks us to do the one thing that we do not want to do!

As with Jeremiah, God sees our whole life. He knew us before we were born and he sees us as we will be when we are in heaven with him. He knows us through and through. His timing is perfect and we need to learn to trust him to speak to us when he chooses to do so. Complaining seldom helps. It is good and right to be honest with God but, in the same way that God replied by confronting Jeremiah directly about his concerns, we need to be prepared for our complaints to be exposed. God wants our hearts and spirits, our enthusiasm and energy —and anything that stands in the way of our giving everything we have to God will somehow be lovingly dealt with and removed.

Do we feel inadequate?
Our own feelings of self-doubt, as well as spiritual attack, can constantly keep us fully aware of our weaknesses. Rather than being problems or barriers to God's working through us, however, these things can become the very things that God wants to use. With his help, we are able to turn weaknesses into stepping-stones—not necessarily removing them from our lives altogether but giving them to God

for him to use and work through as he sees fit. As people around us—especially those who know us well—start to see God working in areas of weakness and inadequacy in our lives, they often become even more convinced of the power of God.

In Jeremiah's case, he was feeling young and inexperienced, but God turned this into a childlike trust and simplicity that allowed God's own words to flow through him into the prevailing culture. What in our lives seems to be a barrier? Lack of confidence? Lack of gentleness? Lack of love for the people around us? Lack of patience? Lack of practical skill in certain areas? Lack of support? Lack of finance? Or maybe even a lack of belief that God really does want to use us?

We need to be honest about our feelings, asking God to take each one and use even these weaknesses to show his provision, guidance and love more widely.

Do we say and do only what God is asking of us?
Jeremiah had an ability to speak out only that which God showed him. He left God to interpret and apply the words as he saw fit. Do we do the same? Or are we keen to help God out, to reinforce what he is saying by adding our own words and interpretation?

Jeremiah was a prophet and, like him, many Christians today sense God speaking to others through them, via visions, pictures or words. This is a normal part of Christian life for many people, with some Christians receiving particular anointing and gifts in this area Jeremiah was trained by God to speak out. What training is available to us, to help us develop the gifts that God has given us?

God may speak to us when we are alone or in church, when we are at home or at work. Jeremiah teaches us the importance of listening to God and then being faithful to that—and only that—which he tells us. If, for example, we have a growing sense that God is calling us to work with young children at church, it is right to take note of that, to start to pray about it and maybe to see if opportunities arise to get involved in a local children's group. We should not make the assumption, though, that the calling is necessarily for now, that it must be in relation to a particular church or that it has to be worked out in a particular way. Sometimes God speaks gently in whispers over many years and it is only later that we start to see how the practicalities of the call are to be worked out.

Sometimes we might sense that God is speaking to us during a church service and feel that, like Jeremiah, he may be giving us something that should be shared. This, too, needs to be tested and checked. We should submit our conviction to the church leaders in whatever way is appropriate in our particular church. If it is agreed that the impression should be shared with the whole church, it is vital to say only that which we see or hear. The temptation to add an interpretation of our own can be enormous but that is seldom, if ever, helpful.

What can we learn from Jeremiah's reaction?

Following the 'J' steps will help us to adopt the lessons we can learn from Jeremiah's reaction to God:

- **Jesus**
- **Just**
- **Joy**

Jesus

If anyone had the right to complain to God, it was Jesus. In the garden of Gethsemane, we glimpse a little of how Jesus was feeling as he approached his death and resurrection: 'My Father, if it is possible, let this cup pass from me; yet not what I want but what you want' (Matthew 26:39).

He makes it clear that although he does not want to face the future, he is determined to put what God wants for him before his own feelings. Part of his calling was to be put to death so that we might be set free from our sin. Surely, there has never been such a difficult calling to anyone—after all, Jesus was fully human as well as being God, and as such was capable of feeling fear and panic just like the rest of us. Yet he went through this experience without once protesting his innocence.

When God calls us to something, we never know for certain how it will work out in practice. We may think that we understand but we cannot see the whole picture. If God asks us to face difficult challenges, there will be a good reason for that. Sometimes we may come later to understand why we were called to go through certain things; but sometimes, we do not find out the reasons. God is God and we need to learn how to say with Jesus, 'Not what I want but what you want.'

Just

Jeremiah teaches us the importance of the 'Just' factor. We need to do that which God is asking us to do—just that and no more. When we start to hear God speaking to us, and particularly when he starts to call us to something that we can begin to see unfold around us in very practical ways, it is vital that we train our ears and our spirit to be accurate. We have all been made in the image of God and therefore we are all creative, imaginative, dynamic human beings. This provides us with a wonderful ability to think big, to have vision. Yet the temptation can be to pick up the threads of God's call as they start to emerge and run with them into a future that we ourselves create, rather than sitting with the threads by our feet, waiting for God to pick them up and create something beautiful and ready for us to step into.

Stress is a growing feature of everyday life, both inside and outside the church. One of the reasons for this may be that some of us have not yet learned to be 'just' people. Many of us take on more than God is actually asking us to do. The result of this can be conflicting priorities, less energy for the tasks that God does want us to do and a sense of failure and inadequacy as we struggle to give our best to everything we have become involved in.

God put Jeremiah through a training programme, asking him to say what he saw and then rewarding him with praise when he got it right. Perhaps we can ask God to do the same with us. We need to learn how to listen to God, praying for the discernment to know when and how God is at work around us. Keeping a journal or prayer diary where we can note the little things that we sense God saying to us can be a helpful thing to do in this respect, as we will have a written record of the steps through which God has taken us.

Joy

Joy is one fruit of the Holy Spirit. As we ask for more of the Holy Spirit to guide us into our calling, we will experience joy. This is not a warm, fuzzy feeling of happiness that comes and goes but a deeply satisfying gift that comes with the contentment of knowing that we are being obedient to the will of God and doing what he asks us to do. Jeremiah knew that God had not only called him but was also going ahead of him every step of the way. All Jeremiah had to do was to follow where God led. It is this expectation that God can and will continue to use us, speak through us and equip us that keeps us going in the long term. Jeremiah's ministry lasted for nearly half a century; God has long-term plans for our lives, too.

Questions for personal consideration or group discussion

1. Have you ever undertaken a task for which you felt under-qualified and inexperienced? What happened? How did you feel about taking on such a role? How did it turn out in the end?

2. Looking back, can you see signs of how God has trained and equipped you, preparing you for a task that you were later to accept?

3. Childlikeness is a quality highly valued by God. What signs of childlikeness do others, who know you well, see in you?

4. Are you able to do just that which God asks you to do—no more, no less? Have you ever suffered from stress? Could this be due partly to having taken on more than God was asking you to do?

5. When things get difficult for you, are you able genuinely to say with Jesus, 'Not what I want but what you want'?

Moses—A man of argument

Key verse

But Moses said to the Lord… 'O my Lord, please send someone else.'
EXODUS 4:13

Suggested reading: Exodus 1—4

Once upon a time, there lived a chicken. It was just an ordinary, everyday kind of chicken. Each morning it left its home and went for a walk—out across the fields, down the hill, along the riverbank and back through the forest. One day, as it was out walking, it came upon an egg, just sitting there on the ground. 'Well,' thought the chicken, 'I have nothing better to do today, so maybe I'll just sit here on the egg for a while and see what happens.' After a short time, there was a tap-tap-tapping and out popped a baby bird. But this was not a baby chicken. It was a baby eagle.

The chicken adopted the baby eagle and looked after it as though it were its own. Each day the two of them could be seen walking out across the fields, down the hill, along the riverbank and back through the forest. One day, as they sat for a while to rest by the riverbank, the baby eagle looked up, and there, soaring way above the place where they were sitting, was a wonderful, graceful bird.

'Wow!' said the baby eagle. 'What's that?'

'That,' said the chicken, 'is an eagle. It is one of the most amazing creatures that God has ever made.'

'Wow!' said the baby eagle. 'If only I could be like that.'

'Ah,' said the chicken, 'but you are just a chicken, like the rest of us.' And off they went home.

Day after day, the baby eagle would stop and look up as far as his eyes would take him and he would stare in wonder at the

eagle flying above him. Then one day, as they set out for their
walk on a particularly sunny day, the baby eagle... died.

End of story. It is not a story with a happy ending. But one, as we will discover later, that perhaps would have helped Moses in his encounter with God, had he heard it!

Moses had, perhaps, the most unpromising start to life of any character in the Old Testament! Born into a Hebrew family at a time when the king of Egypt had decreed that all boys born to Hebrew women were to be killed, he came into the world amidst fear, panic, secrecy and terror. Determined that she would do all that she could to keep her son alive, his mother, Jochebed, hid him for the first three months of his life until that became no longer viable. Then she took a basket, made it waterproof and left her son in the basket by the river— leaving her daughter, Moses' sister Miriam, to keep watch and see what happened. When Pharaoh's own daughter found the baby, Miriam suggested finding a Hebrew woman to look after the child. She ran back to Jochebed, and Moses was then reunited with his mother.

It was not until he was older that Moses received his name. He was called Moses 'because... I drew him out of the water' (Exodus 2:10). There is some debate as to whether Jochebed or Pharaoh's daughter named him, and whether he had another name as he was growing up is not clear. What is certain is that at some point his identity changed. Most of us, even if we have little else to fall back on, at least have a name that we can relate to. Moses' very identity was in question.

His problems did not stop there, however. When he came across an Egyptian beating a fellow Hebrew, Moses killed the Egyptian and hid him in the sand. As if that was not bad enough, he realized the very next day that his secret was out, and it was not long before Pharaoh himself heard what had happened. At that point, fearing for his life, Moses ran away.

Then God called him. If ever we are tempted to believe that God calls only sin-free, faithful, Christian men and women who come from secure family backgrounds, we should remember Moses. A murderer with an identity crisis, who grew up in an atmosphere of secrecy, having to pretend that his mother was his maid! What a man to be called by God!

The calling of Moses

Yet God did indeed call Moses. Of all the callings outlined in the Bible, it is perhaps in the calling of Moses that God shows his most persistent, patient nature.

It started while Moses was going about his everyday business. Working for his father-in-law, Moses was responsible for looking after the sheep. One day, while out in the fields, he noticed that a bush which had been burning for a while was not burning up. As he stepped forward to take a closer look, he heard God speak to him. Instantly Moses recognized the voice and responded to the calling of his name with a positive 'Here I am' (Exodus 3:4). As God confirmed his own identity to Moses, awe set in and Moses hid his face. God then outlined the problem—the Israelites were in trouble and God wanted to help them. He was sending Moses to Pharaoh.

We can understand Moses' reluctance. Pharaoh was the very person Moses had run away from. As soon as Pharaoh's name was mentioned, Moses objected. At first he pleaded inadequacy: 'Who am I that I should go to Pharaoh, and bring the Israelites out of Egypt?' (Exodus 3:11)

God dealt with this excuse in the same way as he handled Jeremiah's insistence that he was 'only a boy' (Jeremiah 1:6). The antidote to feelings of inadequacy is to be reassured of God's presence in the midst of the task, but whereas Jeremiah accepted this, Moses did not. God responded, saying, 'I will be with you; and this shall be the sign for you that it is I who sent you: when you have brought the people out of Egypt, you shall worship God on this mountain' (Exodus 3:12).

Moses then starts his series of 'What ifs?' Firstly, he is afraid of being tested by those to whom he goes. What if the Israelites ask him to name the God who sent him? At that time, in that culture, many gods were recognized and each one had its own name. Who would Moses say had sent him? God tells him: 'I am who I am' (Exodus 3:14). This was a highly significant reply, an answer that in one phrase encapsulated the true might and purity of the holy God, as well as simultaneously providing Moses with a powerful answer to anyone who challenged the authority by which he would later speak out. God continues to speak, giving detailed instructions, and telling Moses to go and assemble the elders in order that they might hear what God is saying.

But then comes another 'What if...?' from Moses. 'But suppose they do not believe me or listen to me?' (Exodus 4:1) Like many of us, Moses had no desire to be seen as a fool! What if he did as God asked, only to discover that no one listened to him? God answers in a powerful way—by giving Moses three miraculous signs that he will personally be able to demonstrate in front of all the people: turning his staff into a snake, making his hand leprous and, if necessary, even turning the water of the Nile into blood! Many Christians today would be quite content if God demonstrated only one of those miracles as a sign of their calling, but all three together were still not enough for Moses.

Moses tries another objection. God is asking him to go and speak, yet Moses cries, 'O my Lord, I have never been eloquent, neither in the past nor even now that you have spoken to your servant; but I am slow of speech and slow of tongue' (Exodus 4:10). However sympathetic we might be to Moses' situation, it really does seem as though he is running out of excuses here! Having been brought up in Pharaoh's own household, it is unlikely that Moses was inarticulate (and he certainly had little difficulty in finding the words to object to God's call!) but even if he were, that is no excuse. God deals with this swiftly: 'Who gives speech to mortals? Who makes them mute or deaf, seeing or blind? Is it not I, the Lord? Now go...' (Exodus 4:11–12).

In one last-ditch attempt to get out of the job, Moses says what was perhaps really on his mind all along: 'O my Lord, please send someone else' (Exodus 4:13). He simply does not want to do what he is told!

Until this point, God has gently, clearly and directly answered every objection Moses has put to him. Suddenly, there is a change and we are told, 'Then the anger of the Lord was kindled against Moses' (Exodus 4:14).

The basic problem was that Moses did not trust God. He felt that God was asking him to do something that was just too difficult. It was perhaps the one and only thing that he was afraid to do. In the end, God had to send Aaron along with Moses to get the job done.

Eagles or chickens?

What does the calling of Moses have to do with the story of the baby eagle? The 'what if…?' factor! The baby eagle spent every day asking, 'What if I could become like that graceful bird soaring above the ground? If only I could.' It had a dream, an ambition, an aim. But it failed to reach its full potential in life because it listened to the chicken, who mistakenly thought that the dream was unobtainable. Yet its 'what ifs' and 'if onlys' were at least positive ones.

Moses, on the other hand, was full of negative 'what ifs': 'What if they don't believe me? … What if they ask me your name? … What if my inability to speak gets in the way?' These negative 'what ifs', stemming from his fear and insecurity, paralysed him. The only way Moses could be spurred into action was by being placed alongside the obedient, trusting Aaron.

Confronting our own 'Ifs'

We can all be heard to say 'What if…?' or 'If only…' from time to time. Some of the most commonly heard sayings in churches include:

'*If only I had more time*, then I would read the Bible… pray more… get involved in church.'

'*If only I had more money*, then I would tithe… give to charity… pay off my debts.'

'*If only I were single*, then I could work as a missionary… be free to travel… make more friends.'

'*If only I were married*, then I would be happy… have children to disciple… offer hospitality.'

'*If only God spoke to me like he seems to speak to other people*, then I would do whatever he told me to do.'

Unlike Moses, the apostle Paul learned the key to overcoming his 'what ifs'. He says in the letter to the Philippians, 'I have learned to be content with whatever I have' (Philippians 4:11).

The challenge to us today is to try to adopt the eagle's vision of seeing and trying to reach the full potential of life as it could be, while at the same time being realistic about present circumstances and accepting them without complaint, but rather with a growing content-ment. Above all else, we need to learn from the experience of Moses that complaining and thinking of all the negatives that might happen achieves nothing. God is God and he will patiently encourage us to the tasks he has ordained for us to do. All we do by refusing to accept them is to incur his anger and to water down his blessings.

How can we receive a call as directly as Moses?

We all hear and experience God in different ways. Even if Moses was reluctant to be called, he certainly received a clear and direct calling from God. Why? Why him? Are there lessons that we can learn from Moses that might enable us to hear the call of God in our lives a little more clearly? God spoke to Moses at a particular time in his life and, by looking at the situation in which he found himself, we can observe and adopt for ourselves the following helpful hints:

- **Making the most of what we have**
- **Observant**
- **Sounds familiar**
- **Everyday routine**
- **Sense of responsibility**

Making the most of what we have

Moses knew that Pharaoh had found out that he had killed a man and, as a result, Pharaoh had vowed to kill him. In an attempt to escape with his life, he ran away. He ran to Midian. We are told that this is where Moses settled, eventually getting married and working for his father-in-law. Regardless of why each of us lives where we do—whether it was clear, positive guidance from God that led us there, or whether, like Moses, we were forced to escape for some reason and landed there seemingly by accident with little intention of staying long-term—it is important that we make an effort to settle into the place where we are. Moses made the most of his time in Midian, and although he was there only for a comparatively short time, he wasted no time in getting to know people, building a family and working hard.

God speaks to us when we are settled and giving our all to the people and tasks around us. If we look at the Gospels and explore the miracles Jesus performed, all of them show that miracles happened when ordinary people, like you and me, had given their all; when they had made the most of the situation in which they found themselves. Would Jesus have fed the five thousand if one little boy had not given all that he had for his lunch that day? Would Jesus have turned the water into wine if the host had kept back bottles of wine for himself rather than giving all that he had to his guests? Wherever we are, whoever we are, we have things to be getting on with today. If we accept the things that we already have, and work at them with all our energy and enthusiasm, then God may choose to do with us as he did with Moses, and speak to us about new opportunities.

Observant

The starting point for Moses in hearing the call of God was, to say the least, unusual! He saw a bush burning. In itself, there was nothing unusual about that; in the intense heat of the desert sun it is quite common for dried-up bushes to ignite and burn. But Moses kept an eye on the bush—maybe just to check that the fire did not get out of control and pose a danger to the flock. As he looked, however, he noticed that something was different. Something was happening that was different from normal. This bush was not burning up.

Why is it that many Christians today report that God speaks to them most clearly at times of difficulty or crisis—maybe after an accident or illness, redundancy or divorce? The experience of Moses would indicate that it is when unusual things start to happen around us, things that we had not expected or anticipated, that we look and listen a little more closely. When our normal routine is disturbed, we start to ask the question, 'What is going on here?' When good things start to happen around us—we have a new job, we move to a new home, we develop new friendships or receive a hefty pay rise—we may give thanks to God but we seldom seem to listen to him as clearly and as carefully as we do when things go wrong.

We need to ensure that even while we settle into a routine of everyday life and service, we still attune our ears to the Holy Spirit. What is God saying to us today? As soon as we stop asking that question, God may need to find louder and clearer ways of speaking to us. With Moses, he caused a bush to burn without ceasing. Is there a problem or a situation in our life that does not seem to be abating? Is there an ongoing issue or concern that we can see out of the corner of our eye? Maybe that is the very thing that God is using to attract our attention. Try taking a closer look and, just as he did with Moses, maybe God will start to speak to us through it.

Sounds familiar

Did you notice how quickly the conversation between God and Moses progressed?

When the Lord saw that he had turned aside to see, God called to him out of the bush, 'Moses, Moses!' And he said, 'Here I am.'
EXODUS 3:4

God called Moses by name. Moses, though, instantly recognized the voice, as well as his own name, and responded quickly. For any conversation to start promptly like this, the two people concerned have to know each other already. There has to be an ongoing relationship that is sufficiently intimate for them both to recognize each other.

God is more likely to speak to those people with whom he has an ongoing relationship and dialogue. Ignoring him until such time as there is a crisis is not likely to be helpful. How will we recognize the voice of God, if he does speak to us, if for the previous few months or even years we have either ignored him altogether or paid only a cursory glance his way?

Being faithful in prayer and Bible study, getting to know the character of God as well as his commands, will ensure that when he does call, we, like Moses, will be able to recognize his voice instantly, and respond.

Everyday routine

Moses heard God speaking to him whilst he was 'keeping the flock of his father-in law Jethro' (Exodus 3:1). This was the job that Moses had been given, and day after day he would roam the countryside looking after the flock. In other words, God spoke to Moses whilst he was going about his ordinary, everyday business.

Routine is important. From the beginning of creation, God established routine. We need days off, times of sleep, holidays and retreats. But equally we need the routine of work. Even when our work becomes dull and repetitive, God can use it to speak to us. I clearly recall being stopped in my tracks as I vacuumed my lounge one day, when God suddenly spoke to me about training people to pray at events. This has now become a key feature of the work of The Framework Trust, a Christian charity I work with. And it all started during a routine period of hoovering! Of course, God can and does speak to us during special times of retreat and prayer and when we are involved in worship and fellowship with other Christians. But we must not neglect to listen for his voice in the midst of everyday tasks that life presents to us. This is as important to God as our being faithful in collective worship.

Sense of responsibility

It is easy to laugh at Moses' reluctance to act upon the call he received. Excuse after excuse was poured out before God. Whilst we can see in retrospect that God was indeed faithful to his promise to be with him throughout his life, Moses did not have the benefit of hindsight. He was scared—scared for his own life at the hands of Pharaoh. But maybe, too, he could see what an awesome and huge responsibility God was asking him to accept. When God asked him to rescue the Israelites, Moses' only response at first was, 'Who? Me?'

The calling of God comes to us at a price. It is always accompanied by a sense of responsibility that lasts until the task has been completed. If we sense that God is asking us to pray for and help people in a particular part of the world, that may, over time, become something for which we adopt a sense of responsibility. Every last ounce of energy, passion and vision within us may be given over to our task of supporting those people. That is not always easy and, as Moses discovered, it can become a lifelong task.

Are we looking for God to call us to something that is easy to bear? Something that will not cause too much disruption to our lifestyle? Or are we genuinely open to God calling us to anything at all that he deems is right for us? Moses weighed up the pros and cons during the call. Once committed to the task, however, he gave it his all. Maybe now would be a good time for us to weigh up our feelings and concerns, so that when God does speak to us we can give one hundred per cent to the task ahead, saying along with Moses, 'Here I am.'

Questions for personal consideration or group discussion

1. Have you ever been concerned that your background might not be suitable for the task to which God calls you? Perhaps through lack of education or qualification, or through geographical location or surname? What does the story of Moses say to you about this?

2. Have you ever tried to bargain with God? Have you listed only negative reasons as to why you cannot do what he is calling you to do? Why was this? What did you learn from that experience?

3. What are your 'if onlys'? Are they positive—helping to spur you towards a vision or a dream? Or are they negative—becoming stumbling-blocks in your way?

4. Have you ever experienced a 'burning bush'—something unusual happening around you? Perhaps a problem that did not go away? Or a sudden redundancy or bereavement? What did God say to you through this?

5. Would you recognize the voice of God speaking to you as you go about your everyday routine? How would you test the voice to be sure that it was indeed God speaking?

Noah—The silent response

Key verse

Noah did all that the Lord had commanded him.
GENESIS 7:5

Suggested reading: Genesis 6—9

Last year I was offered a virtually free holiday in Japan. A friend who works for an airline had the opportunity to take someone with her as the airline explored a new route for the first time. It just so happened that the time suggested was the one and only free week in my diary and I readily accepted.

As a companion to one of the crew, I spent the week with the airline staff, returning with them to the airport for the flight home. On arrival, the captain was greeted by a local man who was waiting to show him to his plane. As I was unable to travel through the staff security procedures, the captain introduced me to the man and asked him to look after me and to ensure that I was shown on to the plane. The man did not look pleased! 'I look after captains!' he exclaimed. 'I don't look after women!' The captain replied, 'If you don't look after her, I won't fly the plane!'

You can imagine my embarrassment! Nearly everyone in the terminal heard this exchange and reluctantly the man told me to wait where I was and he would return to escort me through security. I waited… and waited. Thirty minutes later, the man still had not returned. Conscious of the fact that by this time there were only about twenty minutes to go before take-off, I figured that I had better do something. So I went to the check-in and handed over my documents. 'Are you the one who is travelling with the captain?' the check-in lady asked. 'Yes, I am,' I replied. 'Oh well, in that case you can have this ticket,' she said, somewhat abruptly, as she thrust a boarding card at me.

When I looked at it, I realized that she had given me the very worst seat. For whatever reason, she had decided that someone who was the cause of such fuss in an airport should be taught a lesson. My seat was at the very back of the plane in the smoking section.

At that point, I faced a choice. I could either argue with her in the hope that she would at least get me into the non-smoking section or I could accept it and pretend that it did not matter. I opted for the latter response—but actually it did matter. I was angry. How dare she treat me like that just because the local man had refused to help me. I was angry with her and I was angry with God for letting it happen. All week I had been treated particularly well because I had travelled with the crew. Why stop now and ruin the end of a perfectly good holiday?

As time was short, I moved quickly but fairly grumpily towards the passport control. As I did so, I heard the voice of the Holy Spirit say, 'All I was trying to do was to give you a free holiday.' I suddenly realized how ungrateful I must have sounded. Here was I, after a great week of first-class accommodation and treatment, all at next to no cost, and I was moaning about sitting at the back of the plane. Silently, I apologized. I started to thank God for what he had given me, rather than moaning about what he had not given me.

I moved on to the plane. As the crew recognized me, they did not even check my ticket and I turned right, walking towards the back. As I moved through the economy section, one of the stewards asked me where I was going. I pointed to my seat in the distance. 'Follow me,' he said. I followed him—through to business class. 'There is a spare seat in here,' he told me. 'Sit there.' I went to sit down, this time giving thanks to God as I recognized that silently giving thanks to him had seemingly changed the situation for the better. As I did so, another crew member came and asked me what I was doing. Assuming that he was about to send me back to economy, I started to pick up my bag. 'Follow me,' he said. I did. He took me into first class. 'You can sit here,' he said. 'Wow! Which seat should I have?' I asked. 'You can have them all,' he laughed. 'There is no one else in first class today.'

Not quite believing what had happened, I put my book on one seat, my bag on another and I sat down on a third. By this time, I really knew the meaning of the Gospel verses that tell us that if we are faithful in the little things, then more will be given to us (for example, Luke 16:10). It seemed that as I had stopped grumbling and started to give silent thanks, God had gradually increased that which I had been given.

But that was not the end of the story. No sooner had I sat down in first class than the captain came out and suggested that I sit in the cockpit! For the whole of the flight back, I had the free run of the cockpit, the whole of first class, seven people waiting on me and more food and drink that I could even begin to contemplate consuming! I wonder what would have happened, though, if I had complained aloud to the check-in girl and continued grumbling? Would God have acted in the same way? I doubt it.

A man of few words

Looking at the call of Noah reveals one startling difference from every other call in the Bible. Noah is silent. If he did speak, the words are not recorded. In fact, the only recorded words we have from him come after he got drunk and awoke to discover that, in his stupor, his nakedness had been discovered and covered up.

When reading passages such as Genesis 6, many of us feel inadequate. If God can be so specific when talking to Noah, why can I not hear him like that?

Make yourself an ark of cypress wood; make rooms in the ark, and cover it inside and out with pitch. This is how you are to make it. the length of the ark three hundred cubits, its width fifty cubits, and its height thirty cubits. Make a roof for the ark, and finish it to a cubit above; and put the door of the ark in its side; make it with lower, second, and third decks.
GENESIS 6:14–16

This is only the start. God goes on to give Noah very specific instructions about which animals to take into the ark, what food to take and which people to take with him. He also warns him that he will send rain for forty days and forty nights, with the specific purpose of blotting out from the earth everyone and everything that God has made.

Yet after all this, Noah did not utter one word. He did not complain, question or argue. He did not seek an explanation, request help or walk away from the task. His response is clearly indicated many times throughout the story: 'Noah did this; he did all that God commanded him' (Genesis 6:22).

There is no doubt that in the story of Noah, as in my example of the way God changed circumstances with my airline ticket, silent acceptance of what God gives to us unlocks far more than we could begin to understand. By being silent and offering no resistance to what God is saying, we allow God to be more specific, to give further instruction and often to give a greater blessing.

Silent faith

The book of Hebrews includes a 'hall of faith'—men and women who had exhibited particular faith in action. Noah is included in this list.

By faith Noah, warned by God about events as yet unseen, respected the warning and built an ark to save his household; by this he condemned the world and became an heir to the righteousness that is in accordance with faith.
HEBREWS 11:7

A silent response often indicates a high level of faith. Hebrews 11:1 explains what faith is: 'Now faith is the assurance of things hoped for, the conviction of things not seen' (Hebrews 11:1).

Noah knew God well enough to know his voice, certain that whatever God asked of him would be for a purpose, and trusting that God's purposes are higher than ours. Noah had always done his best to follow God:

Then the Lord said to Noah, 'Go into the ark, you and all your household, for I have seen that you alone are righteous before me in this generation.'
GENESIS 7:1

They had a close relationship; so much so, that when God asked Noah to act, Noah did not hesitate or think twice about it.

Silent humility

Unlike many of the other characters we have looked at, Noah knew who was boss. God was God and Noah was not going to challenge him. He was simply going to do as he was asked.

There does seem to be a correlation between humility and silence. People who exhibit humility tend to be gentle in nature, not relying on words and argument to prove their case but simply and quietly obeying the word of God. Jesus himself, for example, is noted for not having responded on many occasions when it would have seemed helpful for him to do so:

Then Pilate said to him, 'Do you not hear how many accusations they make against you?' But he (Jesus) gave him no answer, not even to a single charge, so that the governor was greatly amazed.
MATTHEW 27:13-14

The proud, on the other hand, like to question and challenge things they hear, seeking to prove their case whenever possible.

Silent respect

The description of Noah and his faith in Hebrews 11:7 adds an important dimension. It states that Noah 'respected the warning'. Respect is a key aspect of Noah's character. He respected God and all that he said. He also ingrained into his family the need for respect of each other. This was evident not only when all the family obeyed his request to board the ark, but later, when Noah lay uncovered in his tent. Maintaining the respect of their elder relation was the motive for covering Noah's naked body.

After the flood, God commissioned him and his family to 'be fruitful and multiply, abound on the earth and multiply in it' (Genesis 9:7).

Noah continued to obey God and planted a vineyard. Whether by accident or intention, Noah became drunk. He became so drunk that he ended up asleep and naked.

This incident is important. Before we start to imagine that Noah was as godly as Jesus, it is important to realize that he was a normal, fallible human being like the rest of us.

Do we respond as Noah did?

What can we learn from the call of God to Noah? Is it simply a case of not arguing with God or is there more to it?

Have we found favour with God?

There is a commonly held but mistaken belief that if we have found favour with God, life will be wonderful! God will bless us and heal us, protect us and feed us. Of course, God does all those things—but he does them as and when he chooses to do so, not as a reward for our faithfulness. If that were the case, we would be able to earn salvation rather than receiving it by grace.

Finding favour with God means that God can entrust key aspects of his plan to us. This might include entrusting us with painful, difficult, inexplicable things that we find almost too much to bear. Mary, the mother of Jesus, is a good example of this. When the angel Gabriel came to visit her, he said, 'Greetings, favoured one! ... Do not be afraid, Mary, for you have found favour with God' (Luke 1:28, 30).

Whilst there can be little doubt that being called to be the mother of Jesus was a particularly amazing thing, it came with much pain. Mary had to endure seeing her son ridiculed, criticized, humiliated and crucified—a lot to bear for someone who was so highly favoured by God.

Other examples can be seen all around us each day. A faithful Christian, for example, who looks death in the face after much pain, despite seemingly endless prayer for healing, may well have found favour with God; for reasons we may never understand, God may need this person, at this time, in this place, to go through horrendous experiences. We may find it impossibly hard to accept but God does know best. Occasionally, examples of fruit from these situations may be found, such as a neighbour or family member who much later recalls turning to God, having seen the sick person continue to worship God in the midst of such pain.

Noah was saved from the flood, but not until he had been given a very demanding job to do. At over five hundred years of age (the equivalent of being fifty to sixty years of age when aligned to today's expected life span), Noah was asked to build an ark that was 450 feet long. He had to find the animals God wanted to save, determine the right level of food stocks and round up his family. With our modern technology and ability to build vast structures, we can forget just what a difficult task this was. It was physically, mentally and, no doubt, spiritually very draining—particularly in view of the opposition and ridicule that Noah probably faced—and taking into account that he was not a young man.

If we want to find favour with God, we need to give him his rightful place—at the head of every aspect of our lives, not just a little corner reserved for Sunday mornings in church.

Do we do as we are told?

When God asks us to do something, do we actually do it? An interesting example of this occurred just as this chapter was being written.

My office is on the first floor. Builders were asked to come and replace the flat roof directly above the office. I was sitting at my computer as they started work. Just then, the phone downstairs rang and I went to answer it. Within a minute of replacing the handset, there was a huge bang. I rushed upstairs only to see that the whole ceiling and roof had collapsed—right on top of the chair I had been sitting on, on the desk and on the computer. The room was well and truly open to the sky! It was only later, having checked that the workmen were in one piece and having cleaned up a great deal of mess, that I realized that had my friend, Kath, not called me when she did, I could easily have been killed. The next day I phoned her back to tell her what had happened. Kath then told me that all that morning she had been feeling that she ought to phone me, but figured that she did not really have anything she felt was worth saying and had put it off, until the nagging thought that she should phone me came back.

That 'nagging thought' was the prompting of the Holy Spirit, asking Kath to do something. It was not a big job or anything out of the ordinary, but it was a vital task that God needed her to do just at that very moment. Without her obedience in that one small respect, you would not be reading this book!

Much of what God asks us to do seems insignificant. We almost do not realize that it is God who is prompting us to do certain things:

maybe to drive home via a different route, to write a letter, or to make a telephone call. Yet once again, it is important to reiterate that when we are faithful in these small things, God often starts to increase the level of responsibility he gives us.

The 'ARK' principle

Following the 'ARK' principle might help us to hear more clearly God's call on our own lives:

- **Availability**
- **Respect**
- **Kingship**

Availability

Noah made himself available to God. He had an ongoing relationship with God that allowed a specific dialogue about a specific calling to take place when it was required.

Are we making ourselves available to God? We may think that we are—maybe by having a regular time of prayer and Bible study, or meeting together at church or in small groups—but sometimes even these things, vital though they are, can get in the way. The routine can become more important to us than actually listening for God in the midst of everything we do.

It is interesting to note that God spoke to Noah while he was already doing, or had just completed, what he had been asked to do. There is no indication that Noah was having specific prayer times or quiet times when God spoke to him. He was going about his general work. God gave him just enough to enable him to get on with the job in hand: instructions to build the ark came first; then details regarding food to store up; once that was complete, instructions about which animals and people to take on board.

Getting up to date with the tasks we already have would seem to be one key to hearing the next step. Often, we do not want to wait. If God asks us to build an ark, we want to know not only the dimensions but also the destination, what will happen after the water has subsided, what kind of house we will live in later, and so on. But God takes a step-by-step approach. He gives us a little, asks us to be faithful in that and then gives us a little more. We may not know what the long-term result will be, but we can be certain that trusting and obeying God is the best thing that we can ever do.

Respect

Occasionally, members of an older generation can be heard to exclaim, 'People have no sense of respect these days!' Respect for our elders, for those in authority, even for God, is not always apparent in today's generation. Yet when we are tempted to believe that we are living in the most difficult generation that has ever inhabited the earth, it is important to note that in Noah's time the earth was also corrupt and filled with violence. In the midst of total wickedness, Noah was the only human being on the face of the earth that God could find who had faith and total trust in him.

Do we respect God? It seems like a strange question to ask—if God is God, then of course we should respect him. But respect is only realized in practice, not in theory. By responding to God's call without argument or question, Noah exhibited respect for his creator. When God asks us to do something, do we simply get on with it, or do we keep questioning?

Respect for God is obviously vital. But so is respect for other people, particularly family members. Noah taught his family to respect each other, especially across the generations. Are we teaching and modelling that same level of respect in our homes and workplaces, in our churches and communities? The *Concise Oxford Dictionary* defines 'respect' as 'to regard with deference, esteem or honour; avoid degrading or insulting or injuring or interfering with or interrupting; treat with consideration; spare; refrain from offending or corrupting or tempting'.

No wonder one of the ten commandments is 'Honour your father and your mother' (Exodus 20:12). Even interrupting them shows a lack of respect! Respect has to be mutual, with parents respecting children as well as the other way round. Respect is a God-given vital quality, that should be evident in the workplace, home and community, as well as in church.

God knew that Noah respected him and those around him. That was one of the reasons Noah and his family were spared from drowning in the flood, and therefore, one of the reasons why God was able to call him to a very specific job.

Kingship

Not only did Noah place God on the throne of his own life, but God deemed Noah to be suitable to be in charge of the whole earth after the flood. This was partly because Noah submitted his whole life to God and was able to take instruction on a regular basis, with little apparent desire to go his own way; but also because he was hard working, a reliable family man who had his priorities in the right order.

What has God put us in charge of? Most people have some level of responsibility: maybe we are a church or home-group leader, a children's worker or leader of worship. Maybe our responsibility is as a parent, or a child of elderly parents. Maybe we are in charge of a project at work, or it is our responsibility to keep the garden neat and tidy. Maybe we look after a pet or keep a watchful eye on a neighbour. Whatever it is that we are in charge of at any given point in time, we need to be faithful to it. We should fulfil that task, no matter how trivial it seems to us, to the very best of our ability. Within the overall constraints of time, energy and family commitments, we need to make it our priority to serve God as best we can in that which we already have. Then, just as we saw with my airline ticket, God may begin to speak to us about increasing our responsibility.

Questions for personal consideration or group discussion

1. There is a saying: 'Silence is golden.' What does this really mean to you? Can you think of examples when the power and beauty of silence have been shown at their best?

2. How can we teach our children, and the young people who attend our church or live in our community, to respect each other? How can we encourage older members of society to respect younger

people and vice versa? Can you think of examples in your family or work situation where respect has been particularly in evidence?

3. In practical terms, how can you work at being 'faithful in the small things'? Think through all aspects of life—relationships, work, church, finances, home, social life and so on. Are your actions in these areas every weekday in line with your prayers about them on Sunday mornings?

4. What has God given you responsibility for? A family? Children? Parents? A job? A church role? A social activity? Encouragement of friends? Money? Time? How are you faithful to God in each area of responsibility?

5. How available to God are you? Can you recall times when God has spoken to you, or when you have sensed his presence with you, at work as well as at rest?

Paul—A man of passion

Key verse
Now as he was going along and approaching Damascus, suddenly a light from heaven flashed around him. He fell to the ground and heard a voice saying to him, 'Saul, Saul, why do you persecute me?' He asked, 'Who are you, Lord?'
ACTS 9:3-5

Suggested reading: Acts 9

On 30 April 1993, a friend and I went to an aerobics class. On the way home, while we were stationary, waiting to turn right into a side road, a car rammed into the back of mine. My friend desperately tried to open the passenger door but could not do so because the impact had caused the car to concertina up. Some men who were waiting at a nearby bus stop rushed to the rescue and managed to pull the passenger door open, allowing my friend to get out. Meanwhile, I was unable to move. As if by way of comfort, the driver of the car that had hit mine came to the window and casually remarked that he had not been looking where he was going! Eventually I was reached by firemen, who lifted me out of the car and into an ambulance, whereupon I was taken to hospital.

Even after being sent home from hospital, I was in a great deal of pain. Every part of my neck, back, head, front and legs seemed to hurt, regardless of how many or what type of painkillers I was prescribed. I was given a collar to wear and told that I would almost certainly never be completely free from pain again. Carefully I was told that I needed to accept that I would never be able to do sport, dancing, skiing or anything remotely energetic. I was told to rest, keeping as still as possible, until at least Christmas; then, in the new year, a programme of physiotherapy and other treatments would be offered to help me regain as much movement as possible. For someone who travels a great deal and has a very active lifestyle, this was not good news. For the first six weeks, I remained at home, moving only slightly and slowly, and always in a great deal of pain.

When I was in hospital, another friend came to see me. She and her husband provided much-needed practical support at a time when I could do very little. They also started to pray for me and, after a while, they asked if they could come and pray with me. At first, I did not actively encourage this. Although I had prayed for healing for other people on a number of occasions, and had seen a lot of healing take place, my pain was so great that I could not think clearly enough to accept anything at all. I simply wanted to be left alone to lie down!

How good it is to have persistent friends! After about six weeks, I agreed to be prayed with and I met with this couple. Having first prayed with my passenger, who, miraculously, had escaped with almost no physical injury, they then turned their prayer to me. As they started to pray, my pain got worse. It became so bad that they had to stop praying, then wait for it to subside before resuming. Working on the principle that something was happening, even if that only meant that the pain was getting worse, we continued. We prayed, then stopped, then prayed again. This happened a number of times. In fact, this pattern went on for about three hours. Then suddenly, in an instant, all the pain from every part of my body vanished. I jumped up, ran round the room and touched my toes. Despite protestations from those who had been praying not to overdo it in case I hurt myself (where was their faith now?) I knew that I had been totally healed. The next morning I went out and dug the garden, before going for a swim in the afternoon. Not one ounce of pain remained and, in the years since the accident, I have not had a single recurrence of those symptoms.

Many times I have wondered why God allowed that whole incident to happen. Everyone involved already knew God to be capable of instantaneous healing—we had seen him do amazing things on many, many occasions. This was not new to us. So why did God put us through it? We can hypothesize with any number of possible reasons but the fact is that we simply do not know. I was hurt; then I was healed. And we have no idea why.

Saul went through a similar experience. One minute he was going about his everyday business; the next he was totally unable to see and had to wait for three days before having his sight dramatically restored. But in Saul's case, we can see why God allowed these things to happen. It was an event that has changed the course of history as countless millions of Christians through the centuries have benefited from the life and teaching of the man whose name was changed to Paul.

Saul and his encounter with God

If you were going to choose one person to be an influential preacher of the gospel, would you have chosen Saul? The initial description of him as outlined in the Bible gives the impression that he was a most vehement opposer of the disciples and other followers of Christ:

Meanwhile Saul, still breathing threats and murder against the disciples of the Lord, went to the high priest and asked him for letters to the synagogues at Damascus, so that if he found any who belonged to the Way, men or women, he might bring them bound to Jerusalem.
Acts 9:1—2

It would be hard to find someone who was more against the spread of Christianity than Saul was at that time. He had already stood by and watched Stephen being stoned to death and, given the opportunity, he would willingly have seen the other followers of Christ go through similar experiences.

Suddenly, as he was going towards Damascus, he heard a voice ask him, 'Saul, Saul, why do you persecute me?' Saul gave a very interesting reply—'Who are you, Lord?'—to which the answer was given: 'I am Jesus, whom you are persecuting. But get up and enter the city, and you will be told what you are to do' (Acts 9:4–6).

With the guiding hands of those who were travelling with him to help, Saul made his way into the city as directed. After three days as a blind, fasting man, Saul received a visit from Ananias, who laid hands on him. His sight was then restored—both physically and spiritually— and immediately afterwards he became a firm convert to the faith he had previously denounced.

What type of calling was this?

When exploring how this call took place, the obvious point to note is that it is a calling accompanied by signs and wonders. Making someone blind is a fairly clear way for God to make a point! On closer examination, however, this appears to be a calling centred around just two questions: 'Why do you persecute me?' and 'Who are you, Lord?'

All God does is to ask Saul why he is doing the things he is already doing. Did God not know why Saul did these things? Did he need an answer to his question? He is God—he knows everything. Yet he asks the question. Why?

The start of something new often comes when we begin to ask questions about our current situation. Many people who become Christians do so just after they start to ask 'What is life all about?' or 'Is what I am doing now, all there is?' By asking Saul, 'Why do you persecute me?' God is questioning and challenging him. This was no doubt a rare experience for Saul. He was in such a powerful position that few would dare to challenge his authority on a day-by-day basis. Yet God dares to ask a question.

No doubt, too, in his dealings with the followers of Christ, Saul had heard the rumours that people believed concerning the raising of Jesus from the dead. He heard them preaching about it and he would have encountered people who claimed to have seen Jesus with their own eyes after the resurrection. By making the question personal, Jesus in an instant replaces Saul's fear and scepticism with awe and belief. Here was someone who was more powerful than he was. Even Saul, with all his contacts, could not produce a flashing light and a voice from heaven! Instantly he acknowledges this power that is so much greater than his: he may ask with whom he is speaking but he already knows, deep down, that it is the Lord.

Often we expect God to tell us things: to tell us what to do, to tell us how to cope, to tell us what he thinks. Although there are undoubtedly times when he does do this, sometimes God simply asks us a question. He has given us an ability to think, to make decisions, to set priorities and, from time to time, he may simply turn the questions we ask back on ourselves—asking, 'What do you think?' When we do ask his opinion, we may be under the impression that he will tell us to do or say the one thing that we would find difficult, the one thing that we do not want to do. Why is this? God loves us and made us, with all our desires and hopes and dreams. Why would he then tell us to leave those things to one side and to look towards doing something that would deny them? Yes, God stretches us, challenges us and teaches us new things, but he also cares about us and asks us to look at what we are already doing and to that which we would like to do.

Apart from the suddenness of it, this is an unusual calling for two reasons:

- It is a call to faith at the same time as a call to ministry.
- It is a call explained in detail to someone else rather than to Saul himself.

A call to faith at the same time as a call to ministry

The sheer impact that this calling made on Saul was sufficient not only to turn his life around, turning him from a vehement opponent to a passionate follower of the gospel; but it propelled him into a life of active service and mission. Note the description in Acts 9: 'For several days he was with the disciples in Damascus and immediately he began to proclaim Jesus in the synagogues, saying, "He is the Son of God"' (Acts 9:19–20).

Immediately. At once. He started to proclaim the gospel without waiting to be told what to do! He just got on with it. As he did so, we are told: 'Saul became increasingly more powerful and confounded the Jews who lived in Damascus by proving that Jesus was the Messiah' (Acts 9:22).

From the moment he became a follower of Jesus, he acted upon a call to speak out.

What kind of things were we involved in or feeling called to just after we became a Christian? Often these things can give us a clue as to the roles and responsibilities God asks us to adopt later on. Even if for many years we are taken in different directions, we may at some point be drawn back to the things that were there at the beginning.

Within a few weeks of becoming a Christian, I was involved in travelling and telling people about Jesus, often being asked to speak or preach, and frequently using the creative arts in order to do so. After about two years this stopped. At the time, I thought that maybe something was wrong: either I had done the wrong things initially or I should struggle to find opportunities to continue. Neither was right. God had given me a vision and provided a starting point, but then he took me to one side for a couple of years, to teach me and prepare me for more of the same kind of work later on.

As we look back to the time when we first recall being a Christian, we might discover elements of our initial calling or ministry that we have a desire to rekindle. Or maybe there were important lessons and experiences we received at the start of our Christian life that have become a foundation for other things later on.

A call explained in detail to someone else

In all the calls that we have looked at so far, God has met with the individual concerned and asked them to accept his calling. Here the story is different. Although God meets with Saul through a dramatic appearance and brief conversation, the details of the calling he has for Saul are revealed not to Saul himself, but to Ananias.

At no point in Acts 9 does God tell Saul what to do. God outlines to someone else, Ananias, the calling he has for Saul:

Go, for he is an instrument whom I have chosen to bring my name before Gentiles and kings and before the people of Israel; I myself will show him how much he must suffer for the sake of my name.
ACTS 9:15—16

If God did pass this message on to Saul, either directly or by asking Ananias to do so, it is not recorded here. The only reason that Ananias seems to have been told of God's plan, is to help encourage him in the extremely daunting task of going to visit one of the most dangerous men in the city.

In the area of calling, others may be able to discern God's plan for us more easily than we can for ourselves. If we are offered promotion at work, for example, particularly if we had not thought about applying for it, this might be because others can see we have potential that we had not realized was there. If we are approached by a church leader to take on a new or increased responsibility, this may be because someone else can discern a possible calling on us to do this. Many people who go on to positions of leadership or other forms of Christian work testify to the fact that the process started when others approached them and suggested that they consider it. Of course, as with all aspects of calling, these things need to be tested and prayed through, but the role of other people can be crucial.

Passion

Both the unbelieving Saul and the totally dedicated Paul highlight an important characteristic for all Christians—*passion*! Saul's depth of hatred towards followers of Christ was transformed into a torrent of commitment once he realized just whom it was that he had met on the road to Damascus. He was totally wholehearted in everything he did, giving every ounce of energy, enthusiasm and excitement to whatever situation he was in.

Are we the same? Do we give everything we have to the situation in which we find ourselves?

How much we need passion—for Christ, for the people around us, for the calling we have been given! Saul may have been doing the wrong things when God met him; he may have been badly misguided and causing a lot of damage; but it was the passion with which he acted that God saw as a characteristic of great potential. With passion, Paul would later be able to accept suffering as well as plaudits, meet Jews as well as Gentiles, talk with kings as well as beggars.

From Saul to Paul

There is a vast difference between the character of Saul and that of Paul. How was this difference manifested? What can we learn from his experience that will help us as we aim to become passionate, committed men and women of God?

To create Paul from Saul, we need to be:

- **Peace-loving...**   not **Self-centred**
- **Accepting...**   not **Argumentative**
- **Under authority...**   not **Unaccountable**
- **Learning...**   not **Lecturing**

Peace-loving, not Self-centred

Saul's very first question acknowledged the lordship of Jesus. This instantly places the relationship in its right perspective: Saul is subservient to God. Whereas before he had traded on the fact that he was powerful and in control, now he sees his power for what it is—weak, feeble and useless when placed alongside the power of God.

To be peace-loving can mistakenly be seen as a weak characteristic. It carries connotations of giving in to others, of allowing oneself to be controlled; it is submissive. Yet submission can be the most creative of qualities! Submitting ourselves to God allows him to do anything at all with us and, because he is the living God of love, that will always be something that is creative, powerful and in our own best interest as well as that of the people we impact.

Saul knew what power was. He had it. As far as humanity was concerned, Saul had reached a top level of power and control. This generated self-conceit in himself and his ability to achieve his goals. When confronted with real power, however, his self-conceited pride dissolves into a far more powerful feature—submission.

If we want to know God's call for our life, we have to know, as Saul did, what peace-loving submission is really about. We are not robots, doing whatever God asks us to do. We need to become people who freely give our lives to God for him to use as he thinks is best. This is never an easy or a weak thing to do. It is an ongoing daily challenge, to live out our faith actively by placing our every step into the hands of our creator.

God knew what Saul's gifts were. He had an ability to be persistent, to persuade others to do things, to preach passionately against the followers of Christ. Once confronted with the living Jesus on the road to Damascus, Paul had to give up those things. He did not know, when he did so, that God would ask him to pick up the same qualities, albeit in a reshaped and redirected way.

Are we proud of our abilities—the things that we do well? Speaking, maybe, or teaching? Singing or leading worship? Offering hospitality or being efficient with paperwork? Striving to be the very best that we can be is a good thing to do but our hearts and our motives need to be constantly aware of the fact that it is God who gives us these gifts and the opportunities to use them. There is no room for self-conceit. The more we can submit our lives to him, the more we will see him at work in, through and around us.

Accepting, not Argumentative

We might think that with such a dramatic conversion and encounter with God, Paul had no choice but to accept what God was asking of him. God, however, always allows us a choice. Paul may have been convinced of the lordship of Jesus but he could then have chosen to stay at home, secure in his own faith but not set upon converting others. Instead he chose to accept the calling that God had given him.

We tend to assume that most of us will find it difficult to ascertain God's call on our lives. However, there are some people who feel strongly called by God to a particular role or responsibility. For these people, their call may be so strong that it can feel overwhelming and as though there is little choice but to accept.

It is important, however, to realize that there is always a choice. Accepting what God asks us to do is something we can choose to do or not to do. Whether we feel strongly called or not, we need to weigh up the consequences of accepting the thing that we sense God is asking us to do. God sees our motives and the desires of our heart, and Paul urges us, 'Whatever you do, in word or deed, do everything in the name of the Lord Jesus, giving thanks to God the Father through him' (Colossians 3:17).

Saul was catapulted into action from the moment he encountered Jesus, but it was action that stemmed from his willing decision to co-operate with Christ, not something rooted in a feeling of compulsion.

Under authority, not Unaccountable

Saul knew the meaning of accountability. Before the events on the Damascus road, he had visited the high priest for letters that would give him the right to arrest followers of 'the Way'. By doing so, he was submitting to the accepted authorities of the day and working properly within the culture in which he found himself.

As soon as he had been converted, he applied the same principle to his new work. He placed himself under the authority of God by being baptized, and under the authority of the disciples as he spent time with them and learned more about the person he had encountered in Jesus.

Whatever it is that we are called to, it is important that we are accountable. There are various patterns of accountability and many churches and organizations establish structures and support mechanisms that provide encouragement, help and advice alongside accountability. We are always accountable to God, of course, but asking others to question what we do will help to keep us on the right track.

Learning, not Lecturing

Saul was a highly educated man. He spent much his time giving orders to others. Yet when he encountered Jesus for himself, he had to go back to the drawing-board. Instead of lecturing others about the foolishness of 'the Way', and the need to keep away from its followers, he had to learn how to point people towards Jesus.

Almost every type of calling demands learning. Whether it is a new skill, a new culture or new people to work with, we are constantly being brought back to the beginning of what can be a stiff learning curve.

Are we teachable? Are we willing to be taught new things, or do we find security in the things we already know? Are we keen to learn more about our faith, ourselves and our surroundings? There is so much more that God has yet to show us! Whoever we are, no matter how wise, how learned, how many qualifications or years of experience we might have, the fact is that there is always more. And in the same way that God took Saul to one side and gave him a living, learning lesson, so too will he take us. He will lead us on into new things—but only if we agree to co-operate with him.

Questions for personal consideration
or group discussion

1. Have you ever been through a situation that you could not understand? Whether it was a good experience or a difficult one, no matter how you looked at it you could not see a reason why God would allow you to go through it. How did this 'unknowing' make you feel? What did it do to your relationship with God, your relationship with other Christians, and your relationship with people who are not yet Christians?

2. Think back to the time when you became a Christian; what did you most want to do then? Tell others about Jesus? Sing praises to God? Read the Bible avidly? Are you doing the same things now—albeit in different ways? Or has God moved you into different areas or roles?

3. Who are the people whose opinion you respect? Why do you respect them? What are the qualities that make them shine out as people whom you hold in high esteem? Could others see these same qualities in you?

4. How passionate are you for God? For your fellow Christians? For people who are not yet Christians? How can you become more passionate in these areas?

5. To whom are you accountable? At work? In your church roles and responsibilities? In your family? In your community? Why is accountability important and helpful?

Section
two

How to capture your call

Reading about the call of God as experienced by well-known Bible
characters is one thing. Hearing, accepting and fulfilling our own
personal call is quite another. Yet how vital it is that we do!
A sense of calling gives us purpose and vision, keeping our eyes
fixed on the world from God's point of view rather than our own.
It gives shape to our lives and a focus through which to channel
our energy, thoughts and actions. Perhaps most importantly,
a call from God keeps us close to him. We recognize our own
weakness and rely daily on him for continued guidance, strength
and encouragement.

What is a calling?

The term 'call' or 'calling' within the Christian context refers to *that which God is asking us to accept*. Often this is linked to a task, job, role or action related to church activities—such as becoming involved in children's work, leading public intercessions or offering our services as a worship leader. But we can equally be 'called' to become an accountant, hairdresser, full-time parent or child-minder. Sometimes a call has more to do with who we are than what we do, such as being called to exercise patience in trying circumstances. A call can come from God to us as an individual or to us as a family or as a church. It gives us a vision and a sense of purpose and often helps us to understand why we have received the gifts and been through the experiences that we have.

A 'vocation' primarily relates to our employment—paid or otherwise—but the dictionary definition of 'calling' is longer and more varied. It is a word used in a variety of contexts, displaying different meanings. Three of these are as follows:

- **cry, shout, speak loudly**
- **utter a characteristic note**
- **an invitation… from God… to a duty or need**
CONCISE OXFORD DICTIONARY

Interestingly, when combined together, the first two definitions are another way of stating the third. A call or cry from God always carries the characteristics of God. This is why we can always test and weigh any call—primarily by laying it alongside his word as given to us in scripture. If a call comes without the characteristics of God attached, no matter how loudly it may appear to be spoken it is unlikely to come from God.

Note, too, the third definition: a call is an invitation, never a command. God does not force his will on us. In fact, he has gone out of his way to give us free will. We can always decline the invitation.

Many of the biblical characters mentioned earlier refused to accept their calling at first. For a variety of reasons, they were reluctant to step into the call as they received it. But God did not give up on them at the first hurdle. It is true that if we persistently refuse to reach out and take hold of the call of God, he may eventually move on and pass the baton to another, but he is a patient and loving father, not one who bullies his children into accepting his gifts. He allows us time to overcome our fears and concerns and then gently leads us into new areas. If ever we feel *compelled* to accept a call, we should question whether this is something that God truly wants us to do.

Having said that, of course, stepping into a call can be a daunting experience. It almost always incurs change and most human beings naturally find change difficult. But if we begin to hear God asking us to step out, if we test and weigh that call via the Bible and in consultation with other people, if practical opportunities to exercise that call start to open up in front of us, and if we have the courage to trust God for the future, then we have a marvellous opportunity to begin to accept the call of God in our lives and see him at work in, through and around us in new, exciting, dynamic and sometimes painful ways.

Is everyone called or just those in 'ministry'?

There are different types of calling. There is a type of calling that automatically accompanies people who become Christians: *the calling to continue to grow in faith* on a day-by-day level. This is a lifelong calling and one that cannot be completed until we reach heaven. This is an aspect of the Christian life that Paul reiterated many times in his letters. To the church at Colossae, for example, he says: 'As you therefore have received Christ Jesus the Lord, continue to live your lives in him, rooted and built up in him and established in the faith, just as you were taught, abounding in thanksgiving' (Colossians 2:6–7).

How this calling to continue in the faith is worked out will vary from person to person, but this is one very important aspect of calling that should not be overlooked. We all have a job to do in maintaining our own faith and personal relationship with Jesus, regardless of anything else we become involved in. This is a full-time role and every Christian—lay or ordained—is called to work at this important aspect of calling.

A second type of calling is that of *the long-term vision*. This may be related to our job or ways in which we can exercise the gifts God has given to us. People who become Christians at an early age, as children or young teenagers, may have the opportunity to pray through their education and career decisions at the start of their working life. This brings together faith and a desire to hear God's call for their future, with the practical career guidance that is often available within educational environments.

But for others who may have become Christians much later in life, or who through personal circumstances were unable to accept a job or role they would have liked, questions about the long-term vision may be crucial. Many in this situation find themselves frustrated that they are not more involved in 'full-time Christian work' of some kind. Yet God knows exactly where he has placed us. He was still God when we took that job or that responsibility, even if we have only recently come to recognize him as such! No matter where we spend our time, whether that is in paid employment or unpaid activity, we will meet other people. We may be the only Christian those people will ever meet. Our role there is crucial. It is important not to undervalue the opportunities that we have been given. Yes, God may one day move us to something different, but first we need to try to see where and how he is working where we already are.

A long-term call or vision does not have to be restricted to our daily work. We have opportunities to serve in churches and in communities. One important aspect of call is to ask God to show us which role he wants us to have in these areas. For example, we may have a desire to work with children but could never consider changing career to work as a teacher; if so, we could talk to the children's workers at church. Maybe we love reading and have a good, strong voice that could bring Bible readings alive during church services. Why not talk to a church leader and see if we could be involved in this way? Or maybe we know that we have an ability to make people feel welcome—perhaps just by a smile or a kind word. Could there be a role for us as part of a church welcome team? Callings need to be tested. Part of the testing process is to ask others for their opinion. If we approach someone and offer help, we should not become anxious if they turn us away. There may be a number of reasons for this—the time may not be right now but perhaps later they will come back to us. Perhaps we are unaware of additional gifts that others can see in us, and discussion with them may help us a little further along the journey of finding the right role for us.

Exploring our long-term call will help to give an overall direction to our life. It will help us to identify our gifts and abilities and give us opportunities to exercise and grow in these areas.

The third type of call is more *immediate*. We may know that we have a call to grow daily as a Christian and we may even know that in the long term we are called to a particular concern or role, but what if our current circumstances are such that we are unable to exercise our long-term call? Parents, for example, often experience frustration when faced with the realities of bringing up their children and being forced to accept that this may, for a time at least, restrict their ability to do other things. A family bereavement or redundancy may force some people to give up cherished jobs or roles. Clergy, church leaders and missionaries are increasingly experiencing times of stress and burn-out—forced to take a period of leave or recuperation. Far too often these situations are accompanied by feelings of failure and a strong sense of 'what we are not doing'.

The Bible shows us that even the people who are most dedicated to God have times of doing something different. Far from being unfruitful, these are often, in hindsight, key times of learning, growth and rebuilding. When accepted and used positively, these times can be the springboard from which far greater things can be achieved later on. If we were to write a career plan for Moses, would we have started by leaving him in a basket and then giving him away? Or would we have thought to make Saul blind in order to help him see the kingdom of God? God's ways are different to our ways, as Isaiah makes very clear:

For my thoughts are not your thoughts,
nor are your ways my ways, says the Lord.
For as the heavens are higher than the earth,
so are my ways higher than your ways
and my thoughts than your thoughts.
ISAIAH 55:8–9

Perhaps the hardest kind of call to accept, especially in a busy modern culture, is that of waiting—waiting and recuperating; waiting and listening; waiting and doing very little. This can, however, be a valid call. It may not last for ever, but to the person concerned it almost always feels as if it is lasting too long. God knows what we need and there are times when he calls us aside—to be with him, to be with friends or family, to be alone.

God knows all about us. He calls us with all our faults, all our hurts, all our fears, and he calls us as members of families, businesses and communities. But he does indeed call each one of us—to a living, growing relationship with him, to a long-term vision and to an immediate place where we can both give and receive. Calling is for everyone, not just those involved in 'ministry'.

Seven steps to CAPTURE your call

How do we go about capturing our threefold call? There are a number of different aspects to identifying, accepting and stepping into a call, but the following seven steps should provide a starting point:

- **Courage**
- **Action**
- **Prayer**
- **Testing**
- **Unity**
- **Reverence**
- **Expectation**

Courage

Have you noticed how frequently God tells those he is calling not to be afraid?

Then the angel of the Lord said to Elijah, 'Go down with him; do not be afraid of him.'
2 Kings 1:15

'Do not be afraid of them, for I am with you (Jeremiah) to deliver you, says the Lord.'
Jeremiah 1:8

The angel said to (Mary), 'Do not be afraid, Mary, for you have found favour with God. And now, you will conceive in your womb and bear a son, and you will name him Jesus.'
Luke 1:30–31

Shock, surprise and even fear are natural reactions when we start to realize that God is speaking to us. Yet the creator of the universe, the

God who loved us so much that he was prepared to die on a cross for us, that same God is the one who meets with us and asks us to step into new challenges and opportunities. Life is never boring as a Christian! Daily we see God's hand in the things that happen around us and occasionally we gulp with astonishment as he creates opportunities that we had not expected.

Sometimes, the more clearly we hear his call, the more daunting it can be. I remember leaving college and joining a theatre company. I had only been a Christian for a few weeks and did not know the Bible at all well. A friend suggested that I write to a Christian theatre company and apply to join their team. This I did and, following an interview, I was offered a place with the proviso that when I prayed about it, I should sense that God wanted me to accept. I sat down to pray but kept being distracted by the word 'Deuteronomy' coming to my mind. I tried to dismiss it but seemed unable to forget it. I called a friend, who pointed out that this was a book in the Old Testament (I had not at this time even started reading the Old Testament!) and maybe I should read it. As I sat down and started with chapter 1, I soon came upon the following:

The Lord our God spoke to us at Horeb, saying, 'You have stayed long enough at this mountain. Resume your journey, and go into the hill country of the Amorites as well as into the neighbouring regions—the Arabah, the hill country, the Shephelah, the Negeb, and the seacoast—the land of the Canaanites and the Lebanon, as far as the great river, the river Euphrates. See, I have set the land before you; go in and take possession of the land that I swore to your ancestors, to Abraham, to Isaac, and to Jacob, to give to them and to their descendants after them.'
DEUTERONOMY 1:6—8

This seemed fairly clear to me! I certainly felt that I had been in London quite long enough and was keen to leave the city. I called the director of the theatre company and read the verses. He laughed! The first place where the company was booked to work was on the sea coast of Devon. Then it was up to the hill country of Scotland and then, during the following two years, to just about every town and village in between!

It was only later, though, that I really understood the significance of this clear calling. Whilst I loved travelling the country and telling people about Jesus, I found much of the work and the lifestyle incredibly difficult. There were many times when I simply wanted to walk away. It was at these times that the Holy Spirit reminded me of that initial call and how God had asked me to be there. This helped to put everything into perspective, and there is something very therapeutic about being able to say to God, 'You asked me to come, I'm trying to be obedient, forgive me where I've failed and *please* sort out the problems!' Since that time, I have noticed a consistency of pattern—the more clearly God calls me to a task, the more difficult I usually find it.

Calling is frequently accompanied by change. Change is seldom easy and requires a great deal of courage. Moving house, changing job, getting married, accepting a role within church—all can require significant changes and often involve a steep learning curve. God has created the world with order and pattern. Night follows day. Autumn follows summer. Children succeed their parents. We can get used to a daily, weekly, monthly or annual routine. These patterns, with a mixture of work and play, are beneficial and help to keep our lives balanced and fruitful. But God is also a God of surprises! Routine can sometimes become a barrier to hearing and accepting a call from God, as we become so comfortable as we are that we do not even continue to ask if we are still in the right place and doing the right things.

Being prepared to change, to grow, to move, requires courage. We need to place our fears and concerns into the hands of our loving creator; to recognize that God knows the plans he has for us and that they are 'plans for your welfare and not for harm, to give you a future with hope' (Jeremiah 29:11). Trusting God, hearing his call and stepping into the future is often scary but God knows what is best for each one of us and as we offer our fear to him, he gently gives us all the courage, help and encouragement (which is another way of saying that we are being 'empowered with courage') that he knows we will need.

Action

There is a saying that it is always easier to steer a moving train than to start one moving from scratch. How true this is in the area of calling! God is the one who guides us, the one who has plans for us, the one who oversees every aspect of our lives; yet we too have a part to play. If we sit back and wait for a voice from heaven to guide us into a dynamic new lifestyle, most of us are unlikely to do very much. In the same way that learning how to work together with a new colleague, friend or spouse takes time, energy and care, so too does drawing close to God. And that, ultimately, is how we are most likely to hear his call—by being close to him.

Practically, there are a number of things we can do:

Study scripture

As it says in 2 Timothy 3:16–17, 'All scripture is inspired by God and is useful for teaching, for reproof, for correction, and for training in righteousness, so that everyone who belongs to God may be proficient, equipped for every good work.' Getting to know the Bible will help us get to know God himself and to discover aspects of our own character that perhaps we did not even know were there. The Bible has something to say about all aspects of our lives and it is as relevant to us today as it has been to people throughout history. We need to commit ourselves to spending time reading, learning and meditating on the Bible. A systematic approach, with the use of Bible notes or study aids, is often more helpful in the long run, as it avoids the pitfalls that can occur when we pick verses at random to suit our situation.

Pray

Prayer is a vital tool in keeping alive our relationship with God. In the same way that a parent loves to hear their child utter the first words of 'mama' or 'dada', so God loves to hear us call to him. The Bible says, 'The smoke of the incense, with the prayers of the saints, rose before God from the hand of the angel' (Revelation 8:4). Our prayers are going straight to God! He hears every word that we speak, every heartfelt sigh and every prayerful tear or laugh.

Along with prayer, fasting is another helpful way of getting closer to

God. While this can mean giving up food and meal-breaks in order to spend the time in prayer, there are other creative ways of fasting. Could we give up watching a television programme for one hour a day, for example? Or walk to work instead of using the car? However we do it, God sees our motives. He knows that small actions like these can be full of the desire to draw closer to him and, as it says in the Old Testament, 'Those who honour me, I will honour' (1 Samuel 2:30).

Ask

If we want to hear the call of God, we need to ask him to speak to us. We should ask him to show us what he wants us to do—today, this week, this year. We can ask him to bring the Bible alive to us as we read it. We can ask him to teach us all the things that he knows we will need to know for the tasks to which he is calling us. God encourages us to ask him for help and advice. He is our father and longs to give us the things we need. But he will not force himself upon us. He quietly waits until we invite him to come and speak to us.

Create time and space

Sometimes we can live such busy, organized (or even disorganized!) lives that it is quite hard for God to answer our prayers. Would we hear him if he spoke to us today? Or is there too much noise and activity happening all around us? Are our diaries so full that we could not fit him in, even if he asked? Creating a little time, space and often silence can indicate to God and to others, as well as to ourselves, that we are seriously committed to seeking his will and serving him. If our personal situation is such that it is difficult finding a time each day to sit and listen to God, then maybe we can make a point of creating space just once a week, or even once a month. We need to be realistic. Setting aside a three-hour quiet time each day may be great in theory but it is unlikely to work in practice. Creating half an hour each month to complement our ten minutes' daily quiet time might be possible, though. The amount of time, or frequency, is not the issue; the important thing is to dedicate ourselves to being available to God. And when we do find some space, what should happen? Possibly nothing at all! We can pray. We can read the Bible. We can sit and think. Or we can just sit, making ourselves available to God. We should expect him to speak to us but we should not fall into the temptation of telling him how and when he should speak. Many people find that when they start to set aside time to be with God, little appears to happen during those times at first, but maybe later—perhaps when they are driving along the road or talking with a friend—they start to sense the presence of God in a particularly close way.

Seek advice

At some point during the process of capturing your call, it will be important to seek the advice of other people. Jesus took a few disciples with him to all the key moments of his ministry, such as the transfiguration (Mark 9:2) and the garden of Gethsemane (Mark 14:32–33). He took along people who knew him well, who were starting to see and understand what God was doing in and through him, and people who, as far as they were able to do so, would watch and wait with him. Who are the people who know us well enough to help us discern and test our call? Maybe a church or home-group leader, a friend or a family member? The people we meet see us at different times and in different roles. Often they can identify our strengths and weaknesses even better than we are able to do. Our ongoing relationship with God, through prayer and Bible study, is vital but so too are the people around us, including people who are not yet Christians. We need to identify those people with whom we can pray, discuss and discern God's call. If we have a spiritual director, a prayer partner, a co-worker in our church role or a friend or relation, we should ask them for help. No doubt they would count it a privilege to be asked.

Accept gifts

The Holy Spirit brings gifts! Do we know what he has given us? Have we accepted the gifts that we have been given or are we pushing them away? Knowing our gifts can help us to prepare for a calling God has for us—maybe in many years to come. We should read and meditate on the passages in the Bible that talk about spiritual gifts. The following extract is a good place to start. As we read the passage, we should pray that God would show us the gifts that he has for us.

Now there are varieties of gifts, but the same Spirit; and there are varieties of services, but the same Lord; and there are varieties of activities, but it is the same God who activates all of them in everyone. To each is given the manifestation of the Spirit for the common good. To one is given through the Spirit the utterance of wisdom, and to another the utterance of knowledge according to the same Spirit, to another faith by the same Spirit, to another gifts of healing by the one Spirit, to another the working of miracles, to another prophecy, to another the discernment of spirits, to another various kinds of tongues, to another the interpretation of tongues. All these are activated by one and the same Spirit, who allots to each one individually just as the Spirit chooses.

1 CORINTHIANS 12:4–11

Personality

There can be a tendency to undervalue the gifts that we have which are not listed in the Bible. Personalities are a God-given part of our personal style but they are not spiritual gifts. Temperament, talents and skills, along with our spiritual gifts, all help to make us the people we are. God creates us with imagination and creativity, with flair and energy. These are all equally important when exploring aspects of calling. We need to recognize all our strengths and weaknesses. It can be helpful to make a list of the qualities and skills we know that we have or that others have pointed out in us. We should thank God for each one and, in prayer, offer them to him for use as he sees fit.

Look for opportunities

'The word of the Lord came to (Jeremiah), saying, "Jeremiah, what do you see?"' (Jeremiah 1:11)

Immediately after Jeremiah had been called to go and speak as a prophet to the nations, God asked him, 'What do you see?' Of course, this is a vision that Jeremiah saw in his imagination and spirit rather than in earthly reality around him; but there is a sense in which God asks us to look around and see what is there. When we realize that we might be being called to serve as an intercessor, for example, or as a children's worker or as an accountant, suddenly we look at the world around us in a new way. Opportunities to get involved at church as the treasurer, or to change career to become a teacher, may seem to present themselves to us. Often a calling is reinforced in a number of different ways over a period of time. Keeping a note of the Bible verses we keep coming across, the things that people say to us or the church services and sermons that particularly speak to us, can be very revealing. By looking back, we can sometimes see patterns—the same themes recurring. Could this be a gentle call?

Wait

What about those of us who never seem to hear God? Those of us who pray regularly, read our Bibles, serve God as best we can in churches and families, and yet never seem to be sure that we know what God really wants us to do? Guilt can set in, especially when we see others around us receiving a dramatic call, suddenly changing direction and moving on, seeming to leave us behind. But we are not asked to compare ourselves with others. On the day of judgment we will be asked to give an account of what each of us personally has done—not what we have seen our neighbour do. Quite possibly, we might already be in the right place, doing the right things, and God may not need to redirect our lives just now. Being open to hearing God's call is often enough. After all, as long as we are genuinely open to listening, he is quite big enough to be able to speak to us if he wants to! Feelings of guilt need to be overcome. In their place, we need to learn to value what God has already entrusted to us—our children, our homes, our jobs. A few people (I admit to being one!) are called to move frequently, constantly to accept new challenges and, with them, new homes, churches, jobs and friends. Yet those of us who are moved around learn to value highly the people and communities that are called to stay in one place. These people often have the higher calling, a calling that goes unrecognized and seldom praised: the calling simply to be there— maybe remaining in one place all their lives. This provides a stability and continuity that is much needed in an increasingly fast-paced world.

If we are not hearing a calling from God, we should not panic. God knows each one of us and loves us, just as we are. We should keep reading the Bible and praying, doing the things that we are already doing. One day he might speak to us clearly about a complete change in direction or just a slight alteration to our lifestyle. Whichever it is, it will be worth waiting for.

There is much that we can do in order to help discern the call of God in our lives. God will play his part in his time and in his way. We simply need to work at preparing and maintaining the ground, ready to receive his seed of change when it comes.

Prayer

How is our prayer life? Dynamic? Exciting? Vibrant? Or is it more of a duty and a hard slog? Do we receive answers to our prayers almost immediately the words leave our lips? Or do our requests and petitions seem to bounce straight off the ceiling and back to us? We all know that prayer is important—our lifeline to God. It can at times, though, seem difficult and dull, our failings in this area merely adding to our feelings of inadequacy as Christians.

Yet how vital prayer is in the area of calling! Many of us long to hear God speak to us, to know what it is that he would most like us to do. How quickly, though, we become discouraged if we do not receive instant answers. We live in an age where speed is of the essence and the word 'instant' seems to be attached to everything from coffee to the internet. If only we could find a system of prayer, a foolproof method of praying, that would release answers from God quickly and clearly!

But God will not be hurried, or pressurized, or cajoled. He is God. He is a loving Father who waits for his children to come to him and spend time with him. He longs to grab our attention—not always so that he can answer our prayers, but simply to waste time with us! Wasting anything may not be a popular pastime in our environment-friendly culture but wasting time with God, often through prayer, is perhaps one of the most valuable things that we can do. When we find something, or someone, that we love—another person or a hobby—time becomes immaterial. We will happily spend hours just focusing on the object of our desire. And this is how God sees us—even though we may have done many things wrong; even though we cannot love God to the same extent that he loves us; even though we are simple, weak, fallible human beings. Even so, God loves us. Read what he says in Hosea:

It was I who taught Ephraim to walk,
I took them up in my arms;
but they did not know that I healed them.
I led them with cords of human kindness,
with bands of love.
I was to them like those
who lift infants to their cheeks.
I bent down to them and fed them.
HOSEA 11:3–4

So much of what God does for us is unseen and unnoticed; see how the verses in Hosea state that even when God heals us and feeds us we do not know that it is him! Prayer is often the time to notice some of these things. As we spend time recognizing who God is, what he has done and is doing for us, thanking him for the things we have been privileged to receive—then we start to see things from his point of view. Our need to have instant answers to our concerns lessens and we can more readily come to terms with the situation in which we find ourselves.

So how should we pray? And how does our need to hear God call us relate to prayer?

Freedom to be creative

First, it is important to note that each person is unique. There never has been, and there never will be, anyone like you or me anywhere in the world. The relationship between God and each person will therefore be slightly different, and in the same way that it is impossible to tell others exactly how they should and should not relate to other people, so too it is impossible to lay down rigid rules about our communication with God.

I recall hearing a sermon a couple of years after I had become a Christian. The vicar was talking about how awesome God is and suggested that in the same way that we would prepare ourselves to meet with the Queen, or a head of state, so too we should prepare ourselves to pray. He stated that people who had their prayer times while still in bed really had not understood what an important encounter this was and he advocated that our habits should change— no more prayer times in bed! Rather, we should wash, dress and sit formally in the living-room waiting for this most important visitor to meet with us. I thought about this for some time afterwards and I wondered if he could be right. Until that point, I had regularly had an hour or so in the morning praying and reading my Bible in bed. Anxious to follow the advice of a much wiser man, I made the decision no longer to pray when I first awoke, but to get up and have a prayer time later. Disaster! The lounge was full of interruptions and the biggest problem was that the thought of having to leap into action the minute I woke up simply propelled me back into sleep! For weeks I struggled with this and in the end figured that for me, personally, a quiet time in bed where my Father in heaven and I could simply chat to each other was by far the best option.

Another person I know suggests that it is impossible to pray curled up on a sofa; rather, that we should sit upright, both feet on the floor and with legs definitely uncrossed. The theory for this is great—that if we intend to be there for some time, then it can become uncomfortable having our legs crossed. However, this is the advice of a six-foot-tall man—and it is advice that does not work for a woman under five feet tall, who has difficulty in getting her feet to the floor at all when sitting upright in an armchair!

How and where we sit to pray may seem irrelevant, but being forced to accept other people's ways of doing things can be restricting and may end up becoming a barrier to prayer. God wants us to meet with him. He knows our situation—how much time we have, what our homes are like, how many interruptions there are. I believe he wants us to be creative when it comes to planning our times to pray. We need to establish a pattern that suits us and our family situation. Maybe from time to time it will be important to change this pattern but we have to take one day at a time. How much time can we give to God in prayer today? Where is the best place for us to pray? In bed? In the bathroom?

In the car? Walking to work? We must take advice from friends and church leaders and pray that God will show us a pattern of prayer time that is unique to us.

Freedom to adore

Have you ever seen young children waiting to greet their favourite grandparent or aunt? After a long tiring journey, the first question grandparents may hear from their loving grandchildren is, 'Have you brought me a present?' Parents may hastily rush to the rescue, suggesting forcibly that the children at least start by asking how their grandparents are and telling them a little about themselves! They need training in getting their priorities right—and so do we!

Too often, prayer meetings—whether individual prayer times at home, or open church prayer meetings—focus on the requests: 'Please, Lord, do this. Please, Lord, do that.' But we would not encourage our children to do that with relatives, so why should we allow each other to do it with God?

When we have a particular concern—especially if it is something that seems close to God's heart too (such as telling us our calling)—we can be overtaken by enthusiasm to start our prayers by asking God to speak to us. Whilst there is nothing really wrong with doing this, as God loves to hear us ask for the things we need, how much we miss by not spending time simply telling him what we think of him.

When was the last time we told God that we loved him? When was the last time we thanked him for sending his Son to die on a cross for us? When was the last time we simply sat and meditated, letting our thoughts dwell on the empty cross or tomb? Spending time thinking about these things will help us to keep our own concerns in perspective. We will begin to realize that if God can raise Jesus from the dead, our own concerns are simple to him. We will soon remember that it was our own sin that made the cross necessary and we will realize how small and insignificant we are in relation to God.

We need to spend time adoring God. We should tell him how we feel about him—even if we are angry with him just now. He asks us to be honest, not religious; to be real, not a copy of other people.

Freedom to confess

Garrison Keillor in *We Are Still Married* (Faber and Faber, 1989) tells us that in 1976, a major Protestant denomination narrowly defeated an attempt to destigmatize the Prayer of Confession by removing from it all guilt or guilt-orientated references: 'Lord, we approach Thy Throne of Grace, having committed acts which, we do heartily acknowledge, must be very difficult for Thee to understand. Nevertheless, we do beseech Thee to postpone judgment and to give Thy faithful servants the benefit of the doubt until such time as we are able to answer all Thy questions fully and clear our reputations in Heaven.'

We may laugh at this—if we did not too frequently do the same, that is! We know that we are sinners because the Bible tells us that we are. When we do something particularly dreadful and feel guilty about it, then we agree that we are sinful by nature. Yet much of the wrong that we do goes unnoticed. If we judge ourselves by the world's standards, most Christians are not guilty of many wrongs. Yet when we start to look at God, and his standards, then we begin to realize just how sinful we really are. This is why it is vital to spend time adoring God first. It puts our sin into perspective. The little things that the world accepts as being OK may not be acceptable in God's eyes.

- We may not steal large amounts of money from the bank but do we make unauthorized personal telephone calls from the office? Or do we leave work five minutes early, thereby stealing time from our employers?
- We may not covet (envy) our neighbour's house but are we jealous of other people's lifestyles, or the gifts, such as preaching or teaching, that others in our church have been given?
- We may not bear false witness (lie) to the police when we see an accident happen in front of us but do we claim that God has told us things when actually he has not done so? Or do we keep quiet when we know that we should be speaking out?

God has a zero tolerance policy on sin. No sin is acceptable. We need to be honest with ourselves and with God about the sins that we commit, asking for forgiveness and relying on the death and resurrection of Jesus to overcome the sin and its effects.

One of the amazing aspects of God's character is that he chooses to speak to us and use us even when we are sinful. If he chose only to speak to people who were free from sin, he would only ever have spoken to Jesus. Being free from sin is not a prerequisite for hearing God's call. It is, however, something that we should constantly work towards as an everyday part of our faith. The effort we apply to overcoming the sin in our lives can be the training ground on which God prepares us for the tasks he has for our future. People who have battled against addictions of various kinds, for example, can be released by God into using their experiences to help others fight similar problems.

Keeping short accounts with each other and with God raises our awareness of sin and helps us to focus on God's standards, rather than our own.

Freedom to thank

Rejoice always, pray without ceasing, give thanks in all circumstances; for this is the will of God in Christ Jesus for you.
1 THESSALONIANS 5:16–18

Being joyful, praying and giving thanks are commands, not optional extras. We are asked to give thanks in all circumstances, not just when things are going particularly well. This can be difficult at times— especially in tragic circumstances such as bereavement; or in times of financial hardship or illness. Just how are we supposed to give thanks during these times?

No matter what happens to us, no matter how difficult things become, we know that somehow, somewhere, God is working his purposes out. We know that we have a place in heaven and that we have a God who knows our situation, whatever that might be. If nothing else, we can thank God that he has given us an ability to pray, and an opportunity to ask for his help in making us more thankful.

When we are seeking to hear God's call, being thankful is extremely important. Thankfulness makes us focus on the benefits God has given us, the things that he has given us in the past and the things he provides for us today. If we find ourselves in a situation or job or ministry that we do not enjoy, there can be a tendency to seek God's call as a way out, a means of escape: maybe if he calls us to something new in the future, we will no longer have to deal with the problems of the present. Yet being thankful is often a key to seeing God at work.

Jonah ran away from God. He knew what he should have done but freely chose to do the opposite. After being thrown overboard, he was swallowed by a fish and remained there for three days and three nights. As soon as Jonah started being thankful, however, God moved him on:

'But I with the voice of thanksgiving
will sacrifice to you;
what I have vowed I will pay.
Deliverance belongs to the Lord!'

Then the Lord spoke to the fish, and it spewed Jonah out upon the
dry land.
JONAH 2:9–10

Many Christians, today, testify to the fact that once they came to accept the situation in which God had placed them, once they started to thank God for what he had given them, *then* they were moved on. Although at one time they were desperate to leave and change direction, by the time God did move them on they were sorry to go.

Psalm 103:2 tells us not to forget all the benefits of God. If we find giving thanks difficult, we may find it helpful to start keeping a written list of some of the things he has given us, either in the past or in the present. We can add to it times when we have been aware that God has spoken to us—maybe when we first became a Christian, for example. We can then pray through the list, thanking God for each item.

Freedom to ask

Asking God for what we need may seem like the best place to start when we pray, but it really does help to do this after the other aspects of prayer. Asking usually takes two forms: asking God to help others and then asking him for our own provision. Both are equally important.

God encourages us to ask him for the things that we need. It shows our dependency on him and our desire to co-operate with him in prayer as we look for the answers to our prayers.

How we ask for things is important, especially in the area of calling. If we become convinced that we know what we need and what our calling is, there is a danger that we may simply ask God to confirm that we were right all along, when actually he may wish to show us that he had something much better in mind. On the other hand, the Bible encourages us to be specific when we pray, in the knowledge that God is a good Father who longs to give us what he knows we need:

'Is there anyone among you who, if your child asks for a fish, will give a snake instead of a fish? Or if the child asks for an egg, will give a scorpion? If you then, who are evil, know how to give good gifts to your children, how much more will the heavenly Father give the Holy Spirit to those who ask him!'
LUKE 11:11–13

The Bible is full of sound, practical advice! When we decide to pray about our calling, asking for the Holy Spirit is an excellent place to start. The Holy Spirit comes to us with gifts, such as wisdom, knowledge, faith, prophecy and discernment—all vital tools for identifying our call. But there is more. The fruit of the Holy Spirit is love, joy, peace, patience, kindness, goodness, faithfulness, gentleness and self-control —all the qualities that we need in order to maintain our call successfully.

If we want to discover what God wants us to do, we can start by asking for more of the Holy Spirit. We should ask expectantly, certain that Luke 11:13 is true: '…the heavenly Father (will) give the Holy Spirit to those who ask him!'

Freedom to adore

Wait! We've done this bit already! Well, yes, in a way we have. But after confessing our sin, thanking God for all the things that he continues to do for us, asking God to help us in the areas in which we are struggling, what better way of rounding off our prayers than to adore him again?

Just for who he is. And of course, once we have adored him, we will then realize our own weaknesses and want to start the whole prayer cycle again!

Prayer is a significant part of our lifelong calling to maintain and grow in faith. We need to nurture our prayer life actively—maintaining the habit even when it seems difficult, and continuing even when we do not receive instant answers.

Testing

One of the crucial aspects of calling is that of testing the call. How do we know that we really are hearing from God? What if our 'sense of call' is simply a personal desire to do something? How can we tell the difference between God's voice and our own thinking?

Failure adequately to test a call of any kind often stems from fear. But the Bible says, 'There is no fear in love, but perfect love casts out fear; for fear has to do with punishment, and whoever fears has not reached perfection in love' (I John 4:18).

If we truly love God and want him to direct every aspect of our lives, then we will be keen to discover what his will for us is. God always knows best. We cannot see into the future with any degree of accuracy or certainty. Politics, economics and global relationships, let alone our own personal circumstances, can all change incredibly quickly. We may think we know what we will be doing this time next week, next year or in ten years' time, but the reality is that anything can happen. The only one who knows what is to come is God himself. Therefore, God is the only one we can really trust as we step into each day.

The 'Seven steps to capture your call' have built into them a number of ways in which our calls can be tested. First and foremost, any sense of call has to agree with *the Bible*. If it runs counter to the Bible—and that includes the spirit of the Bible's message as well as the letter of the law as written—then the sense of call is almost certainly not correct. Do we know what the Bible says in the areas to which we feel called? If we are sensing that God wants us to be involved in worship, we could create our own thematic Bible study based on aspects of worship. If we feel that we should become involved in the community and local justice issues, we could explore what the Bible says about justice. Or maybe we have an increasing desire to work with young people or teenagers? Again, we could look up verses about children and youth. These will reveal aspects of God's heart about these issues and help us to weigh up whether this really is something we should step into.

At some point, a sense of call will need to be tested with *other people*. Seeking the wisdom and advice of friends or colleagues can be very helpful. Often other people will be able to encourage us as we continue to seek God, praying for us and listening to us as we go through the discerning process. But we should be careful that the people we seek out are not simply people that we believe will agree with us, no matter what. We need wise counsellors, people who genuinely love us and who want God's will for our life, not people who will only look for good things!

Maybe we would very much like to seek the advice of others but feel that to do so would be burdensome to them. Perhaps we genuinely feel that our needs are not as important as those of other people, and that to ask others to give up precious time to pray and talk with us is in some way a waste of their time. This is simply not true! Just imagine if someone else were to approach you and ask you if you could spare some time to pray for them—would you do that? Of course you would! It is a privilege to pray for each other and to help each other. We should not deny others the privilege of praying for us.

Another reason some people give for not seeking the help of others is that they simply do not know whom to ask. It can be difficult at times to find just the right person to ask—especially if there has been a recent change of home, or job, or church and so on. The first thing we can do is to pray about this. We should ask God to show us whom we can talk with. After praying this through, we might suddenly start to remember people we have met in the past, or think of someone at our church, maybe someone that we do not yet know very well. Asking people who barely know us to pray for us can be particularly helpful. If we find that these people start to pray for us in ways that confirm our sense of calling, it is quite likely that God is guiding them to pray like this.

Someone who already knows us and our interests might be tempted to pray more from personal knowledge.

Thirdly, a sense of call will only ever truly be tested by *what happens in reality*. As God opens up opportunities for us to step into, we will start to see fruit. When we work on our own initiative, out of God's will and against any sense of his call, we will not see fruit. Working with God shows signs of his presence—his fingerprints. These may be small and seemingly insignificant but they will be there. Maybe one or two people start to show an interest in Christianity through their contact with us. Maybe someone stops sinning in a particular area because of our example. Whatever it is, the presence of fruit is a sure sign of God at work.

Testing can take many forms. Laying our call alongside the Bible and alongside the opinion of others, and eventually looking for signs of fruit, are just three types of testing. As we move on to explore the relevance of unity, we will uncover other practical ways by which a call may be tested.

Unity

'Again, truly I tell you, if two of you agree on earth about anything you ask, it will be done for you by my Father in heaven. For where two or three are gathered in my name, I am there among them.'
MATTHEW 18:19-20

A sense of calling needs to be tested, as mentioned above, and one way of testing a call is to submit it to other people for their opinion. But is it enough that others agree with us? Does this automatically mean that our sense of calling is correct? Should we work towards our call only on the basis that others agree with us?

Matthew 18:9 has often been used by people who have a strong sense of call. They cling to it, as if to a rock in the middle of a stormy sea, even when there is little sign of God opening the doors into that call. Because one or two others agree that their call may be from God, they assume that this is enough. But this can be very dangerous. Unity is more than simply finding someone to agree with you. Any sense of call has to find unity:

- with scripture
- with personal circumstances
- with skills, gifts and experience
- with those at the giving and receiving ends

With scripture

Any call has to be compatible with God's will as made known through scripture. It is not possible, for example, for God to call someone to work with the occult. In Deuteronomy, God says: 'Whoever does these things is abhorrent to the Lord... You must remain completely loyal to the Lord your God' (Deuteronomy 18:12–13). This level of clarity makes it easy for us to test and weigh certain types of 'callings'.

But in the wrong hands and with the wrong motives, scripture can be used to back up the most tenuous of theories. Take Matthew 18:19–20, for example:

'Again, truly I tell you, if two of you agree on earth about anything you ask, it will be done for you by my Father in heaven. For where two or three are gathered in my name, I am there among them.'

What does this verse really mean? It is often quoted in prayer meetings and church services to encourage us that when we meet together to pray, God will take special note of our prayers. It is used as a faith-builder and to spur us into communicating with our Father in heaven. All of that is good and right and helpful. But if God is with us when we meet together, does that mean that he is with us in a lesser way when we are alone? And if he is particularly keen to encourage us to meet in twos and threes, is there less of God when we meet in home-groups of ten or twenty, or as a whole congregation of fifty or one hundred or one thousand?

To truly understand this passage, we need to put it into context. Matthew 18 starts with the disciples asking Jesus, 'Who is the greatest in the kingdom of heaven?' (Matthew 18:1) The rest of the chapter is a series of sayings, helpfully guiding us towards an understanding of the answer to that question. In particular, verses 15–20 need to be seen as one passage. In verse 15 Jesus says, 'If another member of the church sins against you, go and point out the fault when the two of you are alone. If the member listens to you, you have regained that one. But if you are not listened to, take one or two others along with you, so that every word may be confirmed by the evidence of two or three witnesses.'

Did you note the number of people involved? Two or three. Someone sins and you go to talk to him or her. That makes two of you. If the person does not listen, you need to take along a witness. There are now three of you involved. This is how the passage progresses until Jesus says, 'For where two or three are gathered in my name, I am there among them' (Matthew 18:20). This is not a passage about a cosy kind of unity where we all agree to ask God for things we want. This is a serious, hard-hitting passage about dealing with sin. And when we take sin seriously and determine to help each other overcome the effects of sin in our lives, *then* God will be with us in an especially close way.

Why is this so important to God? Verse 18 shows us: 'Truly I tell you, whatever you bind on earth will be bound in heaven, and whatever you loose on earth will be loosed in heaven.' Sin has eternal consequences—on earth and in heaven. It is vital to God that sin is defeated and he looks favourably on those who seek to work in unity with others and with him to overcome sin and its effects. So in answering the question raised by the disciples—'Who is the greatest in the kingdom of God?'—Jesus is clearly stating that those people who deal with sin in their lives are amongst the greatest in the eyes of God.

One way of checking that our sense of call is from God is to ask ourself and those closest to us whether stepping into that call would lead us towards, or away from, sin. Even if it is the latter, we still need to remain on our guard. We always need to be prepared to sit down with other Christians, admitting sin to God as well as to each other where it is appropriate to do so, and seeking each other's help in overcoming our weaknesses. Then, Jesus says, 'I am there among (you).'

With personal circumstances
How can a call be in unity with our personal circumstances? The most obvious aspect in this area is that of family responsibility. If we are married, God is unlikely to call us far away from our spouse for long

periods of time. If we are parents, it is unlikely that God will ask us to leave behind our children for large amounts of time whilst we spend all our energy on other things. Why are these things unlikely? Because they go against the word and spirit of scripture.

God is a *holistic* God. Sadly, this is a word that has been taken over by the new age culture that is rapidly spreading through western society. Christians, though, need to grasp the holistic nature of God—recognizing that he is interested in every aspect of our lives and not just the more obviously 'Christian' parts.

Yes, God may call us to serve him in a church role of some kind. Some of us may be called to work in a recognized 'full-time' capacity, perhaps as a church leader or counsellor, missionary or musician. But all of us are born into families and communities. We have homes and friends, hobbies and jobs, neighbours and responsibilities. And God has given us all of these things—not just the more obviously holy bits!

When we start to sense a call towards something—a role, a country, a church—that will inevitably mean a call away from other things. We need to ask ourselves whether it is really right to leave behind that with which we are already concerned, as well as asking whether or not we are heading in the right direction.

Many of the examples of calling experienced by biblical characters testify to the fact that God prepares his people over many years. Moses spent forty years in the desert before seeing the land that God had promised him. Paul had to wait three days as a blind, fasting man, before God set him free for a purpose. Even Jesus had to wait thirty years before being able to exercise his unique ministry actively during just a tenth of the same amount of time. In each case, God took time to prepare the individual and the situation to which they were called.

Preparation often comes in unexpected ways. The housebound individual, unable to travel, can be turned into a great intercessor for the needs of the whole world. The childless woman who has stood by and watched others raise families can become a great friend and adult companion to the young when they need someone to turn to. The businessman confronted with a stress-related breakdown can meet with God at the point of real crisis and need, only to discover that God steps in and uses him to help others find the relaxing presence of Christ.

We label many aspects of our lives. We have created titles for our marital status, our jobs, our church roles, our hobbies, our community involvement, our physical status, our religious denominations and so on. When we sense God calling us to something, we then struggle to fit this into each category we have made for ourselves: 'How can I fit in a demanding new role at church when my job is taking more of my time, my family need me at home and I have not had time to see any friends during the last month?' But look at it from God's perspective. Does God really see us as a list of job titles? Of course not! He created us as we are, in our entirety. He calls us only by one name that shows that we belong to him: 'Do not fear, for I have redeemed you; I have called you by name, you are mine' (Isaiah 43:1).

If a calling is truly from God, it will be compatible with our basic commitments as outlined in scripture, such as family life and the need to meet with other Christians for worship and teaching; but it might mean changing or leaving some of the other aspects of our lives, such as moving house or earning less money.

With skills, gifts and experience

We all have skills, gifts and experiences of life that make us able to do a variety of things. In recent years employers have added large sections to job application forms in recognition of the fact that even people who left school without paper qualifications or who have never worked before have skills to offer. The ability to run a home and family shows co-ordination, administration and financial skills. Being involved in local community organisations shows an ability to communicate and relate effectively with others. Nursing a sick relative for many years shows compassion, care and concern. All of these are just as valid as GCSEs or university degrees.

However, having so many skills and abilities can be both a blessing and a curse when it comes to discerning a call. Occasionally, one of us has one particular strength which shines through everything we do; so much so, that when God calls us into a role where this strength is put to good use, others immediately recognize it as God putting the right person in the right place. Many of us, however, are not like that. We are moderately good at a few things but not stunning at anything.

The first thing to do is to recognize that God knows the skills and talents we have—he has after all given them to us by a variety of means. We should thank him for the things we are able to do, whilst at the same time recognizing our weaknesses. God did not intend us to be good at everything, and knowing our limitations can be quite helpful in preventing us from attempting things we are not meant to do.

How willing are we for God to use our skills and experiences? There may be some things that have shaped our character and lifestyle quite significantly but which we would not feel at all comfortable about discussing with other people. On the other hand, these may be the very things that we feel strongly about and have learned much through, and we may find ourselves keen to pass on our insights to others. Experiences such as bereavement, unemployment, singleness, disability and so on have for some people been the springboard to a calling or ministry. Others, having experienced almost identical events, have found that these are the very things that God does not want them to focus upon.

We are all different—unique. We need to be honest with God. We must not bow to pressure from peer groups that like to pigeonhole us into accepting roles simply because they feel we should do so. As we give God our feelings about the things we have been through, he will gradually shape us and use us in the way that he wants to.

With those on the giving and receiving ends

On one occasion, I felt that God was asking me to move to a different town. It would mean leaving behind a home, church, friends and all the things that had become familiar. As part of the testing process, I invited five people who knew me well to come and pray together, specifically asking God to reveal his plan to us. When we first met together, all five people independently stated that their own desire was for me to stay where I was. They did not want me to leave. However, we prayed together for a time and as soon as we stopped, everyone agreed that while their individual human inclination was to encourage me to stay, they all felt that they needed to let me go, as God indeed did want me to move.

This experience was important for a number of different reasons. First, it meant that as a body of people—individuals from different churches—we were able to come together before God to seek his will. It showed unity and a seriousness of purpose regarding the decision that had to be made. Second, as each person had their own opinion overturned, it affirmed to us that the decision to move really was from God and not something that we had dreamed up ourselves. Third, it helped all of us to accept the decision as the best that God intended, not just for me but also for those I was leaving behind and those to whom I was going.

We noted earlier that in order for God to call us to something, he also has to call us away from other things. It is important to note, too, that God prepares not only the place where we are being called to serve, but also those we are about to leave.

Being called away from something is not the same as running away. Running away, as Jonah discovered to his cost, is seldom helpful. Even when situations become incredibly difficult or painful, we need to stay and work through the issues until such time as God calls us to something new. Simply being frustrated with our job, our church or our ministry is not sufficient reason on its own to leave. We need to ask ourselves 'Where does God want me to be?' and 'What does God want me to learn in the present circumstances?'

Having said that, when God does call us to something, we often have to leave behind friends, jobs, homes and ministries. That can be hard—especially as we say goodbye to people we have worked with and grown to love. In an ideal world, we would have been training up people to take over from us as children's leader, community worker and so on, but that seldom seems to happen in reality. We need to trust that God will supply people to fill our shoes when we move on, as well as trusting that God will open new doors for us elsewhere. Occasionally, people are reluctant to move out of a role until they can see someone standing by ready to take over from them. Practically, of course, many jobs do need to be done on a regular basis but this can be used as an excuse to overstay in a role. Again, we need to ask God where he wants us to be and trust him to provide.

When we do move on, it is encouraging to note that often we are moved to churches, towns and jobs where we find that we have developed just the right skills for the current needs. I vividly recall entering a new church some years ago, to be greeted by the words, 'We've been praying for you!' What they meant was not that they had known I would be coming and had prayed for me personally, but that they had been praying for God to send someone to them with particular experience in one type of ministry. It was an encouragement both to the church and to me to discover that God had exactly matched their prayers with my limited experience.

Finally, it is important to note that wherever we go and whatever God calls us to, he is likely to develop in us new skills and abilities. He is constantly shaping us on the inside and occasionally calls us to situations where, like Jeremiah, we feel totally under-qualified. But if we continue to keep the dialogue with him open, if we are honest yet at the same time trusting him to provide all that we need, then he calls us to an exciting future.

Reverence

One of the difficulties of exploring a sense of call is that it forces us to focus on requests to God: 'Lord, show me what you want me to do.' There is nothing at all wrong with doing this; indeed the Bible actively encourages us to seek God's will for our lives. However, there is a danger that we can reduce God to a benevolent Father in heaven who is there only to answer our prayers. This must never happen. Yes, God is love. Yes, God created you and me, and he wants the very best for each of us. But at the same time, he is God.

As it says in Hebrews, 'Therefore, since we are receiving a kingdom that cannot be shaken, let us give thanks, by which we offer to God an acceptable worship with reverence and awe; for indeed our God is a consuming fire' (Hebrews 12:28–29). He is a holy and jealous God who deserves to be worshipped with reverence.

However hard we work at trying to uncover the call of God in our lives, no amount of searching, no ministry or role, should ever become more important than simply recognizing who God is. In the same way that Jonah had to learn that God was interested in him for who he was, more than for what he did, so too should we love God for who he is as much as for what he does.

It is God who builds churches, not us. It is God who directs nations, not governments. It is God who reveals himself to our neighbours, not us. Of course, we have a part to play and God is constantly seeking our co-operation in working with him to heal the world but we do need to remember that he is the Lord and his way is perfect:

As for God, his way is perfect; the word of the Lord is flawless. He is a shield for all who take refuge in him. For who is God besides the Lord?
PSALM 18:30–31 (NIV)

Keeping a right perspective is important. Whether or not we know what God wants us to do, we can still praise him. We can simply sit at his feet and trust in the fact that he is perfectly able to call us to something specific if he chooses to do that. Sometimes, he just likes to be with us—not asking us to do anything at all. We should not be anxious to grow in activity; rather, we should be anxious to grow in Christ.

Expectation

There is a well-known story of an inexperienced evangelist meeting, for the first time, a highly-experienced and successful evangelist. He asked for some advice, confessing that he only saw one or two people being converted each time he preached. 'Surely you don't expect people to be converted every time you speak!' said the successful evangelist. 'Oh no!' said the newcomer. 'Well then,' came the response, 'that is precisely the reason you are not seeing more conversions.'

We need to be expectant people. As Christians, we look forward to the second coming, recognizing the urgency of our mission to spread the good news while we can. We can also be expectant that God will speak to us, that he will call us and use us.

Sometimes it feels as though little is happening. We feel as though we are in a rut. Life can become a routine, and sometimes a highly boring one. But somewhere, somehow in the midst of even the most boring day of washing and ironing, paperwork or simple inactivity, God is at work. We may not see him. We may not understand what he is doing. We may not always feel his presence near us. But he is here, and we must cling to the truths of scripture, rather than our feelings, expectantly waiting for him to call us. As in the story of the bridesmaids waiting to meet the bridegroom, or the master in charge of the slaves, he will come to us on a day and at an hour when we are least expecting to meet with him:

'Blessed is that slave whom his master will find at work when he arrives. Truly I tell you, he will put that one in charge of all his possessions. But if that wicked slave says to himself, "My master is delayed," and he begins to beat his fellow slaves, and eats and drinks with drunkards, the master of that slave will come on a day when he does not expect him and at an hour that he does not know.'

MATTHEW 24:46–50

'Ten bridesmaids took their lamps and went to meet the bridegroom. Five of them were foolish, and five were wise. When the foolish took their lamps, they took no oil with them; but the wise took flasks of oil with their lamps. As the bridegroom was delayed, all of them became drowsy and slept. But at midnight there was a shout, "Look! Here is the bridegroom! Come out to meet him." Then all those bridesmaids got up and trimmed their lamps. The foolish said to the wise, "Give us some of your oil, for our lamps are going out." But the wise replied, "No! there will not be enough for you and for us; you had better go to the dealers and buy some for yourselves." And while they went to buy it, the bridegroom came and those who were ready went with him into the wedding banquet; and the door was shut. Later the other bridesmaids came also, saying, "Lord, lord, open to us." But he replied, "Truly I tell you, I do not know you." Keep awake therefore, for you know neither the day nor the hour.'

MATTHEW 25:1–13

Practical activity programme

The following exercises may help in the process of discerning your call. This programme is not necessarily intended to be followed step by step, although you are welcome to do this if you would find it helpful. Rather, by scanning through the following pages you may come across occasional exercises that will provide a focus for your thoughts and prayers.

There are no right or wrong answers to these exercises and everyone who tries them will have different answers. Comparing your results with those of your friends, may provide a basis for prayerful discussion but no more. You are unique and it is God's call for your life that you should aim to hear—not advice on how to become like other people.

If you are asked to help other people discern their call, these exercises might be a useful starting point. It might be particularly helpful to ask the person you are helping to work through a few selected exercises first, then read the rest of the book and then return to the same exercises. The results might be startlingly different!

Whatever your own personal set of results reveal, at the end of this section there is a thirty-day Bible study. This can be used to help you to come to terms with the results and to pray through the issues raised. This final section is perhaps the most important exercise of all and if you do not attempt any of the other activities, do consider spending a few minutes each day for one month on this.

Current roles and responsibilities

What are your current roles and responsibilities? Until we stop to think about it, we can go on collecting job titles and labels until we become so overworked that we near the point of collapse.

On a sheet of paper, draw a pin person—that's you! (If you are a great artist, you could take time to draw a self-portrait!)

On the head of your person, draw a hat. Any style! Any shape!

Now from that hat draw a series of feathers or balloons and on each one write the name of a current responsibility that you hold, such as parent, housewife, worship leader, Neighbourhood Watch co-ordinator and so on.

The total number of roles and responsibilities at .... (insert today's date) is ....

NB: This is a good exercise to return to from time to time. If you are feeling particularly stressed, it might be that your number of roles has increased; if you find yourself easily becoming bored, it might be that there has been a decrease in the total number of roles.

Now list these roles in four categories:

- **those that are work-related**
- **those that are home-related**
- **those that are church-related**
- **those that are play-related**

Are your lists equally balanced? If not, is there anything you can do to help achieve a more even balance?

Current feeding times

This is not a timetable of your meals but an exercise to help you identify when you are fed physically, spiritually and emotionally.

On the **left hand side** in the table below, write a list of the occasions when you regularly find enjoyment and satisfaction, or feel challenged (for example, playing sport once a week, hearing sermons, holidays, spending time with your friends or family). Only include those events that happen regularly (although do note that something that happens just once or twice a year, such as a holiday, is still a regular event).

On the **right hand side** in the table below, write a list of the occasions when you are regularly stressed (such as putting children to bed each night, working to deadlines) or unhappy, or maybe have to give out rather than take in (such as preaching sermons rather than listening to others preach).

Taking in	**Giving out**
1. _____	1. _____
2. _____	2. _____
3. _____	3. _____
4. _____	4. _____
5. _____	5. _____
etc _____	etc _____

Are these lists balanced? Or are you giving out more than you are receiving? Are you working harder than you are playing? Are you relying on a reservoir of Bible knowledge and prayer experience from the past, rather than actively learning and taking in now? What is your personal response to your findings in this exercise?

_____

_____

_____

Current relationships

Relationships of all kinds are important but there needs to be a balance in relationships as much as in our work and other activity. Do you have a spread of relationships—people who depend on you as well as others on whom you rely? Are you discipling and training people? Are you allowing others to teach you new skills?

Jesus had a clear pattern of relationships. There was a close relationship with God, his father; then there were three of the disciples to whom he became very close; then the remaining nine disciples and others such as Mary Magdalene and the family at Bethany; then there was a range of other people whom he touched and met; and, of course, finally the crowds and others he barely knew but who influenced his life (even if it meant he constantly worked to escape them!)

On a separate sheet of paper, draw a small circle. Around that, draw another larger circle, then another, then another and so on. In the centre write the person you feel closest to or with whom you spend the most time. This might be God or it might be a spouse or parent. In the next circle, write the names of the two or three people who are your closest friends (maybe your spouse or children or siblings). Keep working along all the rings. Each outer circle is likely to have a few more names than the circles inside it.

In the space on the **left of the circle**, write a list of the people who depend upon you in some way.

In the space on the **right of the circle**, write a list of the people on whom you depend.

- **Are the lists balanced?**
- **Underline the people in both lists with whom you have a good relationship.**
- **Ask God to show you what to do with any relationships that have a negative influence on you.**
- **Thank God for all the people he has brought you into contact with.**
- **Pray for every person you have listed.**

Previous life experiences

Take a large sheet of paper and draw a straight, horizontal line on it. Divide this line into sections, each one representing five years of your life (if you are twenty years old, make four sections; if you are eighty, make sixteen sections).

Draw a box above the line, and write in any momentous events—good or bad—that you recall: bereavement, job changes, house moves, new friends and so on.

Then draw a cross above each age at which you recall feeling either particularly close to God or particularly far away. (Put the cross near the bottom line for times when you felt far away and near the top of the page for times when you felt close to God.) Link up the crosses with a line.

Example:

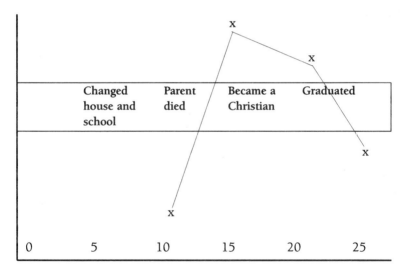

- What does your diagram show you?
- How has your faith been shaped by the events that have happened to you?
- Are any patterns emerging?

Spiritual gifts

Slowly read the following verses:

We have gifts that differ according to the grace given to us: prophecy, in proportion to faith; ministry, in ministering; the teacher, in teaching; the exhorter, in exhortation; the giver, in generosity; the leader, in diligence; the compassionate, in cheerfulness.
ROMANS 12:6–8

To one is given through the Spirit the utterance of wisdom, and to another the utterance of knowledge according to the same Spirit, to another faith by the same Spirit, to another gifts of healing by the one Spirit, to another the working of miracles, to another prophecy, to another the discernment of spirits, to another various kinds of tongues, to another the interpretation of tongues.
1 CORINTHIANS 12:8–10

Pray through each gift listed below. Ask God to show you what each gift means and how it relates to you. Ask him to remind you of times when he has given you any of these gifts (there may only be one or two occasions and it is unlikely that you will be able to recall experiences related to each gift). Pray that he would continue to pour out his gifts on you, giving you just the right opportunities to serve him and the people around you.

- **Administration**   1 Corinthians 12:28 (NIV)
- **Apostleship**   1 Corinthians 12:28
- **Craftsmanship**   Exodus 31:3–5
- **Discernment**   1 Corinthians 12:10
- **Encouragement**   Acts 15:32
- **Evangelism**   Ephesians 4:11
- **Faith**   1 Corinthians 12:9
- **Giving**   Romans 12:8
- **Healing**   1 Corinthians 12:9

- **Helps**   Romans 12:7
- **Hospitality**   Romans 12:13
- **Intercession**   Romans 8:26–27
- **Interpretation of tongues**   1 Corinthians 12:10
- **Knowledge**   1 Corinthians 12:8
- **Leadership**   Romans 12:8
- **Mercy**   Romans 12:8
- **Miracles**   1 Corinthians 12:28–29
- **Prophecy or Preaching**   Romans 12:6
- **Shepherding**   Ephesians 4:11–13
- **Speaking in tongues**   1 Corinthians 12:10
- **Teaching**   Romans 12:7
- **Wisdom**   1 Corinthians 12:8

Spiritual work, rest or play?

Do you notice more opportunity to exercise your spiritual gifts more frequently at home, church, work or play? In the table below, note examples of when you have been able to exercise spiritual gifts.

	Work	**Church**	**Play**	**Home**
Administration				
Apostleship				
Craftsmanship				
Discernment				
Encouragement				
Evangelism				
Faith				
Giving				

	Work	Church	Play	Home
Healing				
Helps				
Hospitality				
Intercession				
Interpretation of tongues				
Knowledge				
Leadership				
Mercy				
Miracles				
Prophecy/ Preaching				
Shepherding				
Speaking in tongues				
Teaching				
Wisdom				

- What has this exercise shown you?
- Do you find that you have more opportunities to exercise spiritual gifts in one aspect of your life? Why do you think that this is?
- Do any of the spiritual gifts regularly appear in all four areas of your life?
- What can you do to develop further the gifts that occur most frequently?

Spiritual fruit

Slowly read the following verses:

The fruit of the Spirit is love, joy, peace, patience, kindness, generosity, faithfulness, gentleness and self-control.
GALATIANS 5:22–23

Pray through each type of fruit listed below. Ask God to show you what each one means and how it relates to you. Ask him to help you recall occasions when he has produced these fruit in your life. Pray that he would continue to develop his fruit in your life each day.

- **Faithfulness**
- **Generosity**
- **Gentleness**
- **Joy**
- **Kindness**
- **Love**
- **Patience**
- **Peace**
- **Self-control**

Current church roles

List any church responsibilities that you already have (e.g. tea-maker, welcome team, vicar, treasurer, PCC member):

_____

_____

_____

_____

_____

_____

For each one of the roles you listed, ask yourself the following questions (it may be helpful to write down the answers):

- How do you feel about this role? (Excited? Bored?)
- How long have you had this role?
- How did you first get involved in this work?
- How much training, encouragement, support and oversight do you have for this role?
- Do you have a vision for this role?
- Are you training or discipling others to take over from you eventually?
- What has God taught you as you exercise this role?
- If your role means that you miss church services (e.g. if you are running Sunday School during sermons and worship times), how do you get spiritually fed?

Potential church roles

Listed below are a number of different roles. Most of these are needed in many (though not necessarily in all) churches. Against each aspect of work, tick the box(es) that most closely match your feelings about the role.

	I don't think I have gifts in this area	I do think I have gifts in this area but I don't want to get involved	I do have gifts in this area and I do want to get involved	I think that God might be calling me to get involved	Other response (write details)
Welcoming people					
Praying in the background					
Praying with people / Prayer ministry					
Helping in a crèche					
Working with children aged 3–10					
Working with teenagers aged 11–18					
Working with adults 18+					

	I don't think I have gifts in this area	I do think I have gifts in this area but I don't want to get involved	I do have gifts in this area and I do want to get involved	I think that God might be calling me to get involved	Other response (write details)
Working with older people 65+					
Working with a particular group (e.g. single parents, unemployed, special needs etc)					
Administration					
Bookstall					
Driving / collecting people					
Marketing and PR					
Hospitality					
Reading the Bible					
Teaching					

	I don't think I have gifts in this area	I do think I have gifts in this area but I don't want to get involved	I do have gifts in this area and I do want to get involved	I think that God might be calling me to get involved	Other response (write details)
Leading intercessions					
Listening					
Making decisions					
Handling finance					
Practical DIY / Making things					
Designing posters and leaflets					
Writing (news sheets, prayer lists, drama)					
Artistic talents (drawing, banners)					
Drama					
Dance					

	I don't think I have gifts in this area	I do think I have gifts in this area but I don't want to get involved	I do have gifts in this area and I do want to get involved	I think that God might be calling me to get involved	Other response (write details)
Music					
PA / technical skills					
Gardening and outdoor work					
Sports events (e.g. running summer camps)					
Leading baptism classes					
Helping with marriage preparation					
Other (specify)					
Other (specify)					
Other (specify)					

Potential community roles

This is similar to the 'Potential church roles' exercise.

Listed below are a number of different roles. Most of these are needed in many (though not necessarily in all) communities. Against each aspect of work, tick the box(es) which most closely matches your feelings about the role.

	I don't think I have gifts in this area	I do think I have gifts in this area but I don't want to get involved	I do have gifts in this area and I do want to get involved	I think that God might be calling me to get involved	Other response (write details)
Neighbourhood Watch					
Befriending elderly neighbours					
Helping families with children					
Voluntary work in charity shops					
Magistrates court or special police work					
Education—helping adults to read & write					

	I don't think I have gifts in this area	I do think I have gifts in this area but I don't want to get involved	I do have gifts in this area and I do want to get involved	I think that God might be calling me to get involved	Other response (write details)
Education— becoming a classroom assistant					
Education— joining the PTA or board of governors					
Prison visiting					
Debt counselling					
Other (please specify)					
Other (please specify)					

Information about voluntary work in any of the above can usually be obtained from your local library or Volunteer Bureau (see telephone book for addresses).

Creative outlets

We are all creative (though not necessarily artistic). Sometimes we can be in the right role but unable to be fully creative within it—for example, a highly creative chef may feel stifled by being asked regularly to serve pre-cooked meals in a hurry to an ungrateful family; or a Sunday School helper might prefer to create his or her own material rather than using a prescribed programme.

When are you most creative?

_____

_____

_____

What opportunities are there for being creative in the following situations:

- **in your workplace**
- **in your church role(s)**
- **in your family responsibilities**
- **in your community**
- **in your play time**

If you had more time to be creative, what would you choose to do?

_____

_____

_____

Is there a way in which you can identify more creativity time (e.g. half a day a month to pursue a hobby)?

capture
your
call

A thirty-day Bible study

Day 1: Called by God

Key verse
Then God said, 'Let there be…'
GENESIS 1:3

Further reading: Genesis 1:1—2:3

Consider

The creation story emphasizes the power of God as he called into being the various aspects of the world. God has the ability to call things into being and as creation hears and responds to that call, order is brought out of chaos.

We are part of God's creation. His calling did not stop on the seventh day. God longs to speak to his children—regardless of where we are or what we may have done.

Hearing God speak to us directly can be a daunting prospect. It might result in a changed lifestyle or attitude. Do we really want to hear God speak to us? Do we have fears about what he might say? Are there aspects of our life we would rather he didn't speak about?

Ask

As we start this Bible study, ask God to speak to you and pray that as you read, think and pray, you will receive a greater sense of his call.

Pray

Tell God how you feel about him. Do you love him? Do you feel angry with him? Do you regret not having spent more time with him?

Thank God for his creative power in making you and for all that he is currently doing, as well as for all that he will do in and through you in the future.

Day 2: Called by name

Key verse
Do not fear, for I have redeemed you; I have called you by name, you are mine.
ISAIAH 43:1

Further reading: Isaiah 43:1–3a

Consider

God does not want us to be afraid. He frequently tells us not to fear. In this passage from Isaiah he goes further, confirming that he has saved us. Spend time unwrapping the full meaning behind each word in the verse, particularly in the phrase-outlines below. Add your own thoughts to the following:

I	I, the Lord God, Father, creator of the universe
Have	already done, completed, not negotiable or reversible
Called	named, identified
You	me, _____ (enter your own name)
By	with, via means of
Name	unique identification, special title
You	me, _____ (enter your own name)
Are	still today, right now, ongoing
Mine	belonging to God, his very own

God calls us to work with and for him, to do a number of things in his name. But first and foremost he has called us—that's you and me—by a unique, individual name which shows that we belong to him. Above everything else he is interested in who we are, rather than what we do.

We cannot earn a place in heaven. There is nothing we can do that will make him love us more than he already does. We belong to him because he has redeemed us and called us by name.

Ask

Do I really know and accept that I belong to God?

Pray

Spend time thanking God:

- **that he has redeemed you by sending Jesus to die for your sin**
- **that he has called you by your personal name**
- **that you belong to God**

Day 3: Called by my name

Key verse

Now the Lord came and stood there, calling as before, 'Samuel! Samuel!'

1 SAMUEL 3:10

Further reading: 1 Samuel 3:1–21

Consider

Samuel heard his name being called three times before he recognized that it was the voice of God.

During the war, Morse code operators were in short supply. Interviews were set up and everyone who could understand Morse code was encouraged to apply. One after another, people arrived, signed in and were told to sit and wait until their name was called. When they heard their name being called, they were to go through the door at the end of the room for the formal interview. They waited and waited. Gradually the room filled up with more and more people waiting for their name to be called.

After some time a man came in, signed his name and sat down. Two minutes later he stood up, went to the end of the room and walked through the doorway. When he came out an announcement was made. 'You may now go home. The post has been filled.'

The people were outraged. 'We've been here all day,' they said. 'It's not fair that someone who comes in last is interviewed first and offered the job.' The administrator replied, 'All day long, with the phones ringing, doorbells sounding and people talking, there has been a man in the corner of the room, quietly tapping out in Morse code, "If you can hear this message, walk to the end of the room, go through the door and you will be offered the job."'

Ask

How much do I miss by not constantly listening out for God's voice?

Would I recognize God speaking to me today? How would I know it was God speaking?

Has God ever had to make me stop doing something in order that I might be free to listen to him? Perhaps through an illness? Or redundancy? Or a change in circumstances?

Can I say—wholeheartedly and unreservedly—along with Samuel, 'Speak Lord, for your servant is listening'? Am I willing to hear whatever God might want to say to me?

Pray

'Speak, Lord, your servant is listening.' Spend time listening to God. Write down what you feel he is saying.

Day 4: Called and known

Key verse

O Lord, you have searched me and known me. You know when I sit down and when I rise up; you discern my thoughts from far away. You search out my path and my lying down, and are acquainted with all my ways. Even before a word is on my tongue, O Lord, you know it completely.

PSALM 139:1-4

Further reading: Psalm 139:1-18

Consider

Picture someone you know well. What do they look like? How do they spend their time? What are their hopes? Their dreams? Their fears? Their concerns? God knows the answers to all of the above questions—*about every single one of us*! But he knows far more than this. He knows every thought we have ever had and every word we have yet to speak.

Ask

How does it feel to be known so well? God sees everything about us—the good and the not so good.

Try to recall every word that you have uttered with your tongue over the last twenty-four hours.

Pray

'With it (the tongue) we bless the Lord and Father, and with it we curse those who are made in the likeness of God. From the same mouth come blessing and cursing. My brothers and sisters, this ought not to be so.'

JAMES 3:9–10

God, examine me and know my heart, test me and know my concerns. Make sure that I am not on my way to ruin, and guide me on the road of eternity.

PSALM 139:23–24, NJB

Day 5: Called and consecrated

Key verse

Before I formed you in the womb I knew you, and before you were born I consecrated you.

JEREMIAH 1:5

Further reading: Jeremiah 1:1–5

Consider

I was recently asked to lead a worship event at short notice. The invitation came during a particularly busy period and every attempt to set aside time to prepare was interrupted by a fairly major emergency. Hence, I arrived just a few minutes before the start, feeling totally unprepared. In desperation I knelt down before God and confessed my lack of planning. 'Lord, I'm sorry but I've had no time to prepare for this event.' In the short, quiet stillness that followed, I sensed the Lord reply, 'But I've been preparing for this moment since the beginning of time.'

God knew us before we were even in the womb. He loves us, watches over us, cherishes us, has plans for us. Wow!

Confession is usually based on what we have already done wrong. Thanksgiving usually focuses on the blessings we have received. Our intercessions frequently reflect the current situations we see around us. But here in Jeremiah, God is looking back and to the future—he remembers back to before Jeremiah was born and goes on to his future as a prophet.

Ask

Ask God, via his Holy Spirit, to remind you of times in the past when he has guided you, protected you, trained you and corrected you.

Pray

Spend time now praying into the future. Thank God for all his past blessings, but go on, in faith, to thank him for what he will do, for the plans he has for you and for the eternity you will eventually spend with him in heaven.

Day 6: Called like a child

Key verse

Then I said, 'Ah, Lord God! Truly I do not know how to speak, for I am only a boy.'
JEREMIAH 1:6

Further reading: Jeremiah 1:6–10

Consider

One December evening, a little boy ran home from school in great excitement. He rushed to his mother and immediately told her the good news: 'Mummy, I've got a part in the school nativity play.' His mother was delighted for her son and asked which part he was to play. 'Oh,' he said proudly, 'it is a very important part—I'm to be a piece of paper.' Thinking that she must have misheard, the mother asked the boy again but he insisted that he really had been cast as a piece of paper.

The following morning, the teacher came out to greet them as they arrived at the school playground and the mother thanked the teacher for casting her son in the forthcoming event. 'There's just one thing,' she added. 'I am a little confused about the actual role he has. He seems to think that he is to become a piece of paper.' The teacher laughed. 'That is probably because I told him that I would cast him as the Page.'

How delightfully funny it can be when children misunderstand! Yet as adults we are expected to communicate effectively at all times. Childlike simplicity gives way to adult complexity.

A sense of inadequacy is often the hallmark of someone truly called by God.

Ask

What is God calling you to be? A parent? A helper? A leader? A speaker?
Complete the following:

I sense that God is calling me to be _____

_____

_____

How do you feel about that? Excited? Delighted? Scared? Unprepared?

Pray

Talk to God about how you feel. Be honest with him as Jeremiah was.
But like Jeremiah, hear what he also says back to you: 'Do not be
afraid... for I am with you.'

Day 7: Called—but what if...?

Key verse

Moses answered, 'But suppose they do not believe me...'
EXODUS 4:1

Further reading: Exodus 3:1—4:1

Consider

Moses launches into his 'What if?' list with God! 'But suppose this happens? Or what if that happens?' What power there is in that tiny word 'if'!

Great visionaries see it as a word of hope and encouragement, powerful enough to spur them on to break new ground:

'What if we could feed every person in the world...?'

'What if no one had to live in poverty...?'

'What if we could cure every illness...?'

On the other hand, many of us use the same phrase to lock ourselves into fear and disillusionment:

'What if my house is broken into...?'

'What if I am attacked...?'

'What if I am made redundant...?'

Recent studies show that more people in Britain are paralysed by the fear of crime than are ever actually affected by it.

Ask

Moses used 'What if...?' as an excuse. We need to recognize our fears and concerns but courageously step out, trusting God to be with us in all we do. Ask God to reveal your own 'what ifs' to you. List them as they come to mind.

Pray

Tell God your personal 'what ifs'. Confess your feelings of inadequacy and ask for his help in overcoming them.

Day 8: Called for help

Key verse
Then Jonah prayed to the Lord his God from the belly of the fish, saying, 'I called to the Lord out of my distress, and he answered me; out of the belly of Sheol I cried, and you heard my voice.'
JONAH 2:1-2

Further reading: Jonah 1:1—2:10

Consider

Despite having had the privilege of hearing God speaking to him earlier, it was only when he got into real difficulties that Jonah deigned to call out to God.

Many of us are like Jonah. We say that we want to hear God calling us, yet when he does, we panic and run away. We can then get into real difficulty—finding that there is no way out, except to call on God.

If I had been thrown into the sea and then swallowed by a big fish, I would probably assume that the fish had been sent by the enemy to make matters worse. Yet the Bible is clear: 'The Lord provided a great fish to swallow up Jonah' (1:17). Surely the Lord could have brought a second boat with a friendly, understanding crew alongside Jonah, allowing him to be taken to the shore in comfort. Why go to the extreme of finding a fish to swallow him?

Jonah knew the reason. It was only when he was in 'distress' that he was prepared to call on the Lord and ready to hear his answer. Sometimes it is much harder to hear and respond to the Lord when life is comfortable. Times of difficulty can prove to be key times of sharpening our spiritual senses.

Ask

Have you ever heard God calling you but wished you hadn't? Maybe he wanted you to move house, change job or challenge someone close to you about an aspect of their lifestyle.

- **What happened?**
- **How did you react?**
- **How did God respond?**

Pray

Are there aspects of your life which are difficult at the moment? If so, make Jonah's prayer (2:2–9) your own. Cling especially to the following phrases:

'You listened to my cry.'

'I will look again towards your holy temple.'

'You brought my life up from the pit.'

'Oh Lord, my God…'

Day 9: Call someone else

Key verse
But he (Moses) said, 'Oh my Lord, please send someone else.'
EXODUS 4:13

Further reading: Exodus 4:2–17

Consider

Moses was being sent by God to Pharaoh to rescue the Israelites—a task which seemed to require someone of great eloquence. Yet Moses claimed that he had 'never been eloquent' but was instead 'slow of speech and tongue' (v. 10). Even God admitted that Aaron had the ability to speak well—so why not choose him instead of Moses?

What do you feel that God is calling you to? Write it down:

_____

What are the gifts, experiences and skills that will be required in order for you to fulfil that call?

- **Gifts** _____
- **Experiences** _____
- **Skills** _____

Ask

Other people may have more obvious gifts, experiences and skills than you do, yet God is calling you. Are you going to argue with God, as Moses did? Or will you humbly accept your call?

Pray

My grace is sufficient for you, for my power is made perfect in weakness.

2 CORINTHIANS 12:9

Day 10: Called for a purpose

Key verse
Then Job answered the Lord: 'I know that you can do all things, and that no purpose of yours can be thwarted.'
JOB 42:1—2

Further reading: Job 38:1-18 and 42:1-17

Consider
Every park should have a seesaw! What fun they are! Yet how rare it is to see two people who are so equally balanced on one that they can both derive the same amount of pleasure. Usually one person has to do more work than the other. But both are needed for the seesaw to work.

Getting the balance right is difficult. On the one hand we know that God calls us for a purpose; on the other hand he is able to do everything and anything without us. Yet we are the body of Christ on earth.

Ask
Job was a successful and upright man. To the best of his ability, he lived a life pleasing to God. Yet he suffered—suffered badly. What was the outcome of his suffering? He realized just how big God is, and how tiny our very best efforts are when compared to such an almighty God.

Pray

Lord, give me a balanced perspective. Help me to accept your overwhelming love whilst at the same time realizing just how big and all-powerful you are. Amen

Day 11: Called at a cost

Key verse
'Whoever does not carry the cross and follow me cannot be my disciple.'
LUKE 14:27

Further reading: Luke 14:25–34

Consider

It is no accident that this verse follows on immediately from a reference to the family. How we all desire to have an extended family of loving, caring, supportive Christians who are a constant source of warmth, encouragement and joy. Yet how rare this is! Many Christians struggle to live out their faith amidst antagonistic, apathetic or critical family members. Learning how to follow Jesus in this situation is never easy.

In the space below, write the names of close friends or relatives who are not yet Christians:

_____

_____

_____

What are some of things these people have taught you about the cross? About the need for patience? For gentleness? For perseverance?

_____

_____

_____

Ask

Ask God to show you what he has taught you through each person listed. Give thanks for each one. Pray for each person you have named—for their physical, emotional and spiritual needs.

Pray

What then are we to say? Is there injustice on God's part? By no means! For he says to Moses, 'I will have mercy on whom I have mercy, and I will have compassion on whom I have compassion.' So it depends not on human will or exertion, but on God who shows mercy.

ROMANS 9:14-16

Day 12: Called by surprise

Key verse
Nathanael asked him, 'Where did you get to know me?' Jesus
answered, 'I saw you under the fig tree before Philip called you.'
JOHN 1:48

Further reading: John 1:43–51

Consider

On my first visit to the church I now attend regularly, I was introduced
to the vicar simply as 'Terry-Anne'. 'Preston!' he immediately added. 'I
know all about you!'

Isn't it disconcerting when someone we have never met before
claims that they know us? The immediate reaction is to assume that
they must have heard all the negative things and that they cannot
possibly *really* know us.

At one of the most difficult times in my life, a friend sent me a card
on which was written, 'The nicest surprises happen when you least
expect it.' How true! And especially how true when it comes to God. It
is often when we are at our lowest point that he calls us to a task which
seems too difficult, too demanding or too daunting but ultimately
proves to be deeply satisfying.

Think back to the times when you most clearly sensed God speaking
to you—through the Bible maybe, or via a talk.

Ask

How did it feel to realize that God knew all about you and your
situation?

Jesus saw Nathanael while he was under a fig tree. Imagine yourself
sitting under a large tree. Simply sitting. Being still. Watching the world

go by. Then, in your imagination, see Jesus walking towards you. He stops. He looks at you. What does he see? What does he know about you? He knows how you feel—what you are thinking, what you are concerned about.

Pray
Jesus, take me as I am
I can come no other way
Take me deeper into you
Make my flesh life melt away.
Make me like a precious stone
Crystal clear and finely honed.
Life of Jesus shining through,
Giving glory back to you.
DAVE BRYANT

Day 13: Called on trust

Key verse

His mother said to the servants, 'Do whatever he tells you.'
JOHN 2:5

Further reading: John 2:1–11

Consider

Hindsight is a wonderful thing. The Bible gives us a record of the miracles performed by Jesus. Today we know that he is capable of anything. Yet at the time of the wedding in Cana, Jesus had not performed any miraculous sign. How much more amazing it is, then, that Mary should trust him so totally that she is able to say to the servants, 'Do whatever he tells you.'

Read Luke 18:18–25.

Key verse

'Sell all that you own and distribute the money to the poor and you will have treasure in heaven; then come, follow me' (v. 22).

Trust is only really proved during testing. We now move to the rich ruler in Luke 18 who was convinced that he was doing everything right in God's eyes. Even by asking the question 'What must I do to inherit eternal life?' he seemed ready and willing to do whatever Jesus asked him to do. Yet Jesus puts his finger on the one thing the man would find particularly difficult: 'Sell everything you have and give to the poor.' When he heard this, the man 'became sad'.

Ask

Am I prepared to do whatever he asks of me? How would I fare if my trust was tested?

Pray

Be honest with God. Tell him the things you find particularly difficult. Tithing? Honesty? Patience? Loving your neighbour?

Ask for an ability to trust God more and more so that you will eventually be able to say honestly that you will do whatever he asks of you.

Day 14: Called with enthusiasm

Key verse
Simon Peter said to him, 'Lord, not my feet only but also my hands and my head!'
JOHN 13:9

Further reading: John 13:1–10a

Consider

We move from the rich ruler, who had difficulty in doing what Jesus asked of him, to Peter, the over-enthusiast.

Having initially refused to let Jesus wash his feet, he then leaps to the opposite stance and invites Jesus to wash his hands and head as well.

Shortly after declaring that he wants his whole body to be washed by Jesus, Peter finds himself betraying Jesus. Was his enthusiasm misplaced or all for nothing?

It is well worth noting that immediately after Jesus' baptism—which marked the start of his main ministry—Jesus is led into the wilderness.

Many Christians report that following clear callings, or particularly close encounters with God, they almost immediately face a time of difficulty—isolation, loss, illness, abandonment.

Ask

When called by God to a specific task, many biblical characters show signs of reluctance, rather than enthusiasm. Why do you think this is? Is enthusiasm a positive or negative quality?

Pray

Ask for God's protection and for his gentle shepherding throughout any times of difficulty you might face today or in the future.

Thank him for his faithfulness, steadfastness and love during such times in the past.

For surely I know the plans I have for you, says the Lord, plans for your welfare and not for harm, to give you a future with hope.
JEREMIAH 29:11

Day 15: Called together

Key verse
After this the Lord appointed seventy others and sent them on ahead of him in pairs to every town and place where he himself intended to go.
LUKE 10:1

Further reading: Luke 10:1–11

Consider

We live at a time when more people than ever before inhabit the earth and yet more people today than at any other time suffer from loneliness.

Can there be such a thing as a 'Christian living in isolation'?

Jesus modelled different types of relationship:

- his personal times on his own with God
- two or three close friends with whom he shared his innermost thoughts
- a small group of people he discipled: people he taught and to whom he passed on what he knew
- people in the community to whom he spoke openly about his life and work—always pointing them towards God

Some of Jesus' closest friends were the least popular members of society—the outcasts and sinners.

Ask

Do I have a similar pattern of relationships to that of Jesus?

- How active, dynamic and vibrant are my quiet times in prayer and study?
- Who are my closest friends? Do I allow them to see me when I am upset and in trouble or do I only see them when all is well?
- Who am I discipling? Who am I allowing to teach and disciple me?
- Do I make the most of opportunities to talk about my faith with people who are not Christians? How much time do I spend with people who are not Christians?

Does my address book reflect the full spectrum of society, or is everyone in it of similar background and experience?

Pray

Ask God to reveal any needs that have become apparent in the area of personal relationships.

Day 16: Called in pain

Key verse

And the Lord was sorry that he had made humankind on the earth, and it grieved him to his heart. So the Lord said, 'I will blot out from the earth the human beings I have created—people together with animals and creeping things and birds of the air, for I am sorry that I have made them.'

GENESIS 6:6-7

Further reading: Genesis 6:1–8

Consider

Has anyone ever said to you, 'I know how you feel'? When someone has genuinely experienced something similar to that which we are going through, it can be a source of great comfort.

The same God who sends his Holy Spirit to produce joy and peace, the same Jesus who celebrated the wedding feast with wine in Cana, the same creator of all humankind; he, too, had a heart that was filled with pain.

When Jesus saw her weeping, and the Jews who came with her also weeping, he was greatly disturbed in spirit and deeply moved. He said, 'Where have you laid him?' They said to him, 'Lord, come and see.' Jesus began to weep. So the Jews said, 'See how he loved him!'

JOHN 11:33-36

Ask

Ask God to speak to you as you either do, or imagine doing, the following:

Light a candle. Sit for a time and watch it burn. It gives out light and warmth, but always at the expense of droplets of wax. These fall—like teardrops.

Pray

Tell God about the things that cause you pain:

- **bereavement**
- **isolation**
- **loneliness**
- **illness**
- **lack of a sense of identity or self-worth**

Accept God's love for you. He sees your pain. He feels it. He grieves and weeps over it. But he loves you and wants to take you by the hand and lead you—not necessarily away from it but through the pain.

Turn to Hosea 11:1–9 and read it as a meditation while being still before the lighted candle.

Day 17: Called to go

Key verse
'Go therefore and make disciples of all nations, baptizing them in the name of the Father and of the Son and of the Holy Spirit.'
MATTHEW 28:19

Further reading: Matthew 28:16–20

Consider

Ready... Steady... Go!

I love watching athletics. The race itself is always exciting but there is just as much to watch before and after those few seconds of strenuous activity. The athletes on the warm-up track. The concentration on their faces as they take off their tracksuits and see the race-track for the first time. The lap of honour afterwards.

Ready... Steady... Go!

God often seems to use a similar pattern when he calls us to a particular task.

Ready Years of preparation. Eating the right food (Bible study). Drinking enough liquid (being filled with the Holy Spirit). Preparing for every possible scenario before the event itself (prayer).

Steady As we explored a few days ago, there can often be difficult times between the preparation and the sending out. We need to remember our call whilst remaining patient, careful to go in God's time and way, rather than our own.

Go No matter how many years God has taken to prepare us, we almost always seem surprised when he starts to use us!

Ask

How has God prepared, or is God preparing, me for the call he has given me?

Am I waiting for his perfect timing, dragging my feet or struggling to move sooner than he wants me to?

Pray

Thank you, Lord, that there is a time for everything.
Please help me to make the best of every opportunity so that I
am always fully prepared. Help me to wait for your leading
and guiding and preserve me from either dragging my feet or
rushing ahead. Enable me always to do the very best that
I can do in all things. For your glory. Amen

Day 18: Called to wait

Key verse
I wait for the Lord, my soul waits, and in his word I hope; my soul waits for the Lord more than those who watch for the morning, more than those who watch for the morning.
PSALM 130:5-6

Further reading: Psalm 130

Consider
All Christians are called to go, called to act, called to serve and so on. So too, all Christians at one time or another will be called to wait.

Despite clearly being called by his Father to a specific task, Jesus waited forty days in the wilderness before starting his ministry.

Paul had to wait three days as a blind, fasting man before being set free by God.

It is almost always much harder to wait than to go.

Ask
Have you ever sensed God leading you towards some task or place, only to discover that you then have to wait for the call to be fulfilled?

Are you in a time of waiting right now?

Pray
Tell God how you really feel about this waiting time. Confess your doubts ('Did God really say…?')

Ask him to teach you all you need to learn during this time. One of the fruit of the Spirit is patience (Galatians 5:22). Pray that God would fill you more and more with the Holy Spirit so that you will have the patience you need in this or in any future time of waiting.

Day 19: Calling the nations

Key verse
Then he opened their minds to understand the scriptures, and he said to them, 'Thus it is written, that the Messiah is to suffer and to rise from the dead on the third day, and that repentance and forgiveness of sins is to be proclaimed in his name to all nations, beginning from Jerusalem.
LUKE 24:45–47

Further reading: Luke 24:44–53

Consider
Comparatively few people can work out their calling by travelling physically to other nations, yet wherever we are—even on home territory—we are to proclaim the message of the gospel.

Have a look at an atlas (or even a map of the UK). Almost every town and village will have a church or a group of Christians in the vicinity. Pray for one or two areas of particular interest, asking God to:

- **strengthen and encourage the Christians in that place**
- **meet the practical needs of the community**
- **help any missionaries or Christian visitors to the area to have the courage and ability to proclaim the good news of the gospel**

Ask
In order to be able to pass on to others the things Jesus has shown us, we have to know what he is saying. How well do you know the Bible? How much of a priority is it in your diary? Is there anything you can do in order to get to know the word of God more fully?

Your word is a lamp to my feet and a light to my path.
PSALM 119:105

Pray
Father, you have the whole world in your hands. Help me to play the part you have given me. Amen

Day 20: Calling the community

Key verse

Then the woman left her water jar and went back to the city. She said to the people, 'Come and see a man who told me everything I have ever done! He cannot be the Messiah, can he?'
JOHN 4:28-29

Further reading: John 4:1-42

Consider

Evangelism! What a difficult thing to do! But maybe that is because it was never meant to be 'done'. Evangelism is about *being* rather than *doing*. It is about being yourself, but outside the church.

When the Samaritan woman encountered Jesus for herself, it was natural for her to tell others in the community about him.

Ask

How often this week or month have you chatted to those you have met about what Jesus is doing for you?

Pray

Meeting Jesus can be daunting. The Samaritan woman felt as though he knew everything about her. The Bible says that God knows even our thoughts: 'Even before a word is on my tongue, O Lord, you know it completely' (Psalm 139:4).

Confess your sins now to God. Imagine that you are taking a broom and sweeping away every shadowy cobweb: deceit... failure... wrong thoughts...

You are forgiven! As far as the east is from the west, that is how far your sins have been removed from you. To help this amazing fact to become a reality in our hearts and minds, use the following verses as a basis for meditation:

For as the heavens are high above the earth, so great is his steadfast love toward those who fear him; as far as the east is from the west, so far he removes our transgressions from us. As a father has compassion for his children, so the Lord has compassion for those who fear him. For he knows how we were made; he remembers that we are dust.
PSALM 103:11–14

Now pray for opportunities to tell others what God has done for you. Pray especially for your neighbours and the wider community and then go on to pray for the nations.

Day 21: Calling the needy

Key verse
But Peter said, 'I have no silver or gold, but what I have I give you; in the name of Jesus Christ of Nazareth, stand up and walk.'
ACTS 3:6

Further reading: Acts 3:1–10

Consider
Need or greed? Sometimes it is difficult to tell which is the motive. Western culture encourages us to feel that we 'need' the latest style of trainers, designer clothes and genetically modified tomatoes. Any parent of teenage children will acknowledge just how strong peer pressure is when it comes to things their children feel they need.

Here is a story of a man who felt he had a need—perhaps a genuine need for money. Yet Peter doesn't meet that need. He has no money to give. Instead he meets a much bigger need that the man would never have thought could be addressed. Peter reaches out and gives what he can. The man is physically healed and immediately goes into the temple and praises God.

Do we care about the whole person or just bits of someone's life? Jesus was interested in the man's practical needs, physical needs and spiritual needs.

Ask
God is interested in every part of your life. List some of the ways in which you have seen him at work in your life recently:

• **Practically (money, job, home etc)**

_____

- Physically (healing, food, rest times, holidays)

_____

- Spiritually (church, prayer, Bible study, fellowship)

_____

Pray
Thank you, Lord, that you look after every part of me. Amen

Day 22: Calling the Church

Key verse

Then some of those who belonged to the synagogue of the Freedmen (as it was called), Cyrenians, Alexandrians, and others of those from Cilicia and Asia, stood up and argued with Stephen. But they could not withstand the wisdom and the Spirit with which he spoke.

ACTS 6:9-10

Further reading: Acts 6:7-15

Consider

Opposition. Virtually anything which has the hallmark of God upon it attracts opposition. Usually we expect it to come from outside the church and we are prepared to fight the world for what we believe is right. But here, as in many cases, opposition comes from within the church.

There is a fine line between critical and unhelpful opposition and positive testing of ideas. How can we test what people say and do in order to ensure that it is God's work which succeeds?

Stephen did great wonders and miraculous signs among the people and even his greatest critics acknowledged that they could not stand up against his wisdom or the Spirit by which he spoke.

Ask

- Have you ever experienced opposition? How did you handle it?
- Have you ever opposed a person or project? How did you handle it?

Pray

*Father, fill me with the same wisdom and Spirit
that you gave to Stephen. Amen*

Day 23: Calling the sinner

Key verse
But when he heard this, he said, 'Those who are well have no need of a physician, but those who are sick.'
MATTHEW 9:12

Further reading: Matthew 9:9–13

Consider

Recently, I heard a story of a church leader who dressed up convincingly as a dishevelled homeless man. He wanted to see how his congregation would react to such a person and so he went into the church just before the start of a service and sat down. No one sat near him and no one spoke to him. After the service, he went for a cup of coffee. Again, no one spoke to him and if he wasn't very much mistaken, there were a few funny looks and critical glances coming his way.

Ask

Would the reaction have been similar if he had visited my church? Would I, personally, have sat next to this stranger? Helped him find the right book and page? Taken him for coffee and talked with him?

Being homeless, dirty and dishevelled is not a sin. Yet we often react more strongly against such people, who disturb our nice, cosy lifestyle, than we do against sin itself.

Most sin is hidden from everyone except God. Jesus came to expose the sin in our lives and bring it into the light. Just as a doctor has to diagnose the problem before he can treat it, Jesus has to highlight our sinful ways before we can be free.

God knows everything about us. Despite that, he loves us and calls us into the fullness of life with him. We don't get to know him because of how good we are or how much we do in church or in the community. We get to know him because he comes alongside us, whoever we are and whatever we've done.

Pray

Have you ever avoided someone because they made you feel uncomfortable to be with? If so, say sorry to God that you walked away from a beautiful part of his creation.

Confess your own sins to God. Thank him that, as the physician, he can come and heal you. Ask him to do so.

Day 24: Calling the young

Key verse

But when Jesus saw this, he was indignant and said to them, 'Let the little children come to me; do not stop them, for it is to such as these that the kingdom of God belongs.'

MARK 10:14

Further reading: Mark 10:13–14; 1 Samuel 1:21–28 and 3:1–10

Consider

Age was no boundary to Jesus.

Hannah prayed for Samuel before and after he was born (1 Samuel 1:27).

The Lord spoke clearly to Samuel while he was still a young boy. Eli recognized that it was the Lord speaking to him.

Ask

How much do we value young people? Young children under seven years of age? Older children aged between seven and eleven? Teenagers? Adults of various ages? The elderly?

Think of one person you know in each age group other than your own. What have you learned from each one?

How do you feel others see you? Too young? Too old?

'You're as young as you feel' is a common saying. Is it true?

What can adults learn from the children and teenagers in the church? How can we encourage different age groups to mix more effectively?

Pray

Pray for couples who hope to have children, for those who are currently expecting children and for those who already have children.

Pray that you would have the wisdom to recognize the Lord at work in the children you meet, and the wisdom to see the child in each adult and elderly member of society.

Lord, help me to value each child I encounter. Amen

Day 25: Called to receive

Key verse
'Truly I tell you, whoever does not receive the kingdom of God as a little child will never enter it.'
MARK 10:15

Further reading: Mark 10:15–16; 1 Kings 3:5–16

Consider

Today, we continue exploring the theme of children but in a very different way. When he said, '...like a little child' Jesus was referring to the quality of childlikeness. This has to do with inner simplicity, trust and faith rather than age.

Make a list of the signs of childlikeness:

_____

_____

_____

Ask

Do other people see the above qualities in you?

What is the calling God has placed on your life? Do you, like Solomon, feel that you may lack the experience to do the job? Trust God. He chooses the right people for the right job at the right time.

Pray
Father, keep me childlike. Keep me close to you. Amen

Day 26: Called to accept

Key verse
John answered, 'No one can receive anything except what has been given from heaven.'
JOHN 3:27

Further reading: John 3:22–30

Consider
Think back to last Christmas. As we approached the day itself, many of us will have seen a growing pile of presents forming under the tree. Some of them had our names on. When it finally came to the time to open the parcels, we were only able to receive those gifts which had been chosen for us by others.

John points out that God is the giver. He calls each one of us to a unique role. It is important that we accept that which we have been given and do not try to reach out for a different calling.

Ask
No doubt, as the ministry of Christ developed, more people followed him and fewer stayed with John. John's disciples had found it difficult when they saw others following Jesus. Maybe they were jealous? Frustrated? Ready to give up?

How do you feel when you see other people succeeding in areas where you feel you have failed? Jealous or genuinely pleased for them? Are you tempted to imitate their 'style' or way of doing things? Do you feel like giving up altogether? Or do you keep on with the things God has asked you to do?

Pray

'He must become greater; I must become less.'

JOHN 3:30, NIV

Day 27: Called to grow

Key verse

He put before them another parable: 'The kingdom of heaven is like a mustard seed that someone took and sowed in his field; it is the smallest of all the seeds, but when it has grown it is the greatest of shrubs and becomes a tree, so that the birds of the air come and make nests in its branches.'

MATTHEW 13:31–32

Consider

Have you ever watched young children playing with building bricks? Even when they are very tiny, they have the ability and enthusiasm to create huge structures.

When God calls us to be a parent, a homemaker, a business entrepreneur or whatever it might be, we often feel that we are under-qualified—too small, too insignificant. Surely God must have got it wrong—he can't want *me* to do this? How can he use 'little me' to do such a big thing?

Yet place the tiny seed of faith inside a person, feed and water it via prayer, Bible study, fellowship and life's experience, and mighty things can be achieved.

Ask

One of the signs that frequently accompanies someone who is genuinely called by God to a task or role is their feeling of inadequacy at the calling. We often feel useless rather than useful.

Have you ever felt under-qualified for a task God has called you to?

Pray

In your imagination, hear the Lord say to you:

Do not call what I have made useless!
I created you.
I love you.
I am calling you.
Trust me.

Day 28: Called to learn

Key verse
So Philip ran up to [the chariot] and heard him reading the prophet
Isaiah. He asked, 'Do you understand what you are reading?'
ACTS 8:30

Further reading: Acts 8:26–40

Consider

It may sound a simple question to ask, but Philip was questioning the
Ethiopian equivalent of the Chancellor of the Exchequer! Here was an
intelligent, educated man being asked if he understood what he was
reading. Perhaps even more amazing is that the man had the courage to
admit that he didn't!

Do you ever read the Bible aloud in public? Many churches ask
people to take a turn in reading the word of God without checking that
they understand what they are reading. The result is often a confused
and bored congregation struggling to understand what is being read to
them.

Ask

As you read the whole passage from Acts 8:26–40, do you understand
what you are reading?

Imagine that you were in Philip's shoes. How would you have
answered the question, 'Is the prophet referring to himself or someone
else?' (8:34) How would you have started with this question and
explained the good news of Jesus to the Ethiopian?

Pray

Father, please help me to understand what I read in your word. Please give me the courage to ask for help when I need it. Amen

Day 29: Called to pray

Key verse
'But whenever you pray, go into your room and shut the door and pray to your Father, who is in secret.'
MATTHEW 6:6

Further reading: Matthew 6:5–15

Consider

The author Brennan Manning tells a story of a young woman who went to his house to ask if he would visit her father. Brennan agreed and went to visit her dad who was in bed, seriously ill. They entered into conversation and it quickly transpired that the man was troubled because he didn't know how to pray. He said that he had asked his own vicar but the only help he received was to be given a book about prayer. The man had tried to read it but had had to use the dictionary nine times on the first page because it was so difficult. In desperation the man asked Brennan if he could help him learn to pray. Brennan told him to place a chair next to his bed, imagine that Jesus was sitting in the chair and chat to him. The man was surprised that it could be so simple and agreed to give it a try.

Some days later, the young woman called to tell Brennan that her father had died. 'But it was strange,' she said. 'I went to see him, kissed him, laughed at his joke and then went out. When I returned he was dead. The odd thing is, though, that he died leaning out of bed, with his head resting on an empty chair.'

Jesus didn't say 'If you pray' but 'When you pray'. All Christians are expected to maintain an active dialogue with God.

Ask

Am I maintaining an active dialogue with God?

Whilst some people are gifted in leading public intercessions during services, the prayer the Father truly desires is primarily that which takes place behind closed doors—the everyday, normal ramblings of an 'ordinary' person as he or she sits in the bath, does the washing-up or prepares for bed.

No matter what our calling is in terms of role, job or task, we are all called to pray.

Pray

Make the Lord's Prayer your own. Say each line and use it as the inspiration for your own personal prayers.

Day 30: Called to abundance

Key verse
For we are what he has made us, created in Christ Jesus for good works, which God prepared beforehand to be our way of life.
EPHESIANS 2:10

Further reading: Ephesians 2:4–10

Consider
Throughout this study we have explored aspects of God's calling and leading. Each one of us is different. Each one of us has a unique part to play in our place of work, our family, community and church. God calls us when we are weak, sinful, needy and in pain. His call can lead us into difficulties and hardship, and in ways that cost us dearly. Yet above all else, his call frees us to live the life he intended us to live. He comes and calls that we might have life in all its abundance.

Ask
Once again, ask God to confirm your sense of his call on your life:

* **Your role in your family**
* **Your role in your community**
* **Your role in your church**
* **Your role in the world**

Pray
Thank God for making you, shaping you and leading you. Thank him for teaching you, rebuking you, correcting you. Thank him for the past, the present and the future.

Use the words of Ephesians 2 as a basis for prayer and meditation:

But God, who is rich in mercy, out of the great love with which he loved us even when we were dead through our trespasses, made us alive together with Christ—by grace you have been saved—and raised us up with him and seated us with him in the heavenly places in Christ Jesus, so that in the ages to come he might show the immeasurable riches of his grace in kindness toward us in Christ Jesus. For by grace you have been saved through faith, and this is not your own doing; it is the gift of God—not the result of works, so that no one may boast. For we are what he has made us, created in Christ Jesus for good works, which God prepared beforehand to be our way of life.

EPHESIANS 2:4–10